Warship
Construction

Bernard Ireland

Warship
Construction

LONDON

IAN ALLAN LTD

First published 1987

ISBN 0 7110 1594 5

© Bernard Ireland 1987

Published by Ian Allan Ltd, Shepperton, Surrey;
and printed by Ian Allan Printing Ltd at their works
at Coombelands in Runnymede, England

Contents

Preface

This is not a book about naval architecture. It does not list the world's fleets nor does it attempt to cover the full spectrum of the warship world. What it seeks to do is to examine and discuss the reasons for having surface warships in the first place and, once the decision is taken, why it is that the resulting vessels are the way that they are. It attempts, not over-technically, to look at the major influences which are brought to bear to finally create what is one of man's more complex set of compromises. If the book proves both informative and interesting then the effort involved will have been worthwhile.

The author would like to recognise and thank the many people and organisations that have helped along the way, both materially and with advice; the project would not have been possible without them. Particular thanks are due, as ever, to his wife who, from somewhere, found as many hours to devote to the project as the author himself.

Bernard Ireland
Fareham 1985

CHAPTER 1

Reasons for Being

The acquisition and maintenance of a fleet has something in common with a successful marriage; it is not undertaken lightly, it needs a genuine initial commitment which, while altering in character, does not diminish with time and, as the cynic would point out, it is of considerable importance to have a deep pocket.

Warships are acquired for a variety of reasons. Of these one can ignore those that are merely the symbols of vanity of an emergent or oil-rich state as they contribute nothing that is original in concept. Greater maritime powers maintain fleets for the defence of both themselves and their allies, and to act as instruments of the State, underscoring its interests in a multitude of situations up to and beyond the outbreak of actual hostilities.

Such great powers depend upon the sea for their wealth and livelihood; their business is world-wide and linked by the sea lanes which it is in their interests to protect. Their ideals lie in a smooth mercantile flow, operating within internationally recognised laws of the sea. When this situation is upset it is a primary duty of their fleets to reinstate it by any means that may be deemed necessary by the State. Warships designed for these duties tend to be self-sufficient, long-ranged and of general purpose design, traditionally of the cruiser type. Their function is what is often loosely termed 'Sea Control', guaranteeing the use of the sea for those purposes required by the State and its allies.

The other side of the coin are sizeable fleets operated by states that have little or no maritime tradition. They do not depend upon seaborne trade and, indeed, may be self-sufficient. Their reasons for maintaining maritime forces are complex but based either on a fear of suffering at the hands of a maritime state or a jealousy of the global influence that these same maritime states apparently enjoy, together with aspirations, overt or covert, toward gaining something of a like standing. Either of these cases may well involve the neutralisation of the rival state's maritime interests in furtherance of their own and they are in the business of what is usually termed 'Sea Denial'. The turn-of-the-century Germany of Kaiser Wilhelm II was an example of a state hungry for greater influence in the world, and the Soviet fleet of today has progressed beyond the stage necessary

merely to secure its boundaries and is also changing its character. Indeed the rapid development of Russian naval strength since 1945 affords an example of existence due initially to a need to counter real or imagined threats to the State and then, having achieved this stage, to provide the means of pursuing its interests, mainly doctrinal, ever further world-wide. Balanced only by limitations in technology and finance, the single-minded purpose of the State, possibly only under totalitarian ideals, has produced a bewildering succession of warship types, their programmes frequently overlapping. This process is worth a brief study.

During the so-called 'Cold War' of the decade or so following the end of World War 2 the Soviets consolidated what might be termed 'Fortress Russia', behind the wide buffer zone of what were to become the bulk of the Warsaw Pact countries. Having recently suffered the latest of the invasions from the West, they worked to ensure that it would never happen again, though apparently morbidly certain that the West had this in mind. Limited by technological and capital resources, the Soviet Navy of the Stalin era had to be developed in order to meet three major requirements:

(a) To counter the danger of the West's proven capacity for amphibious landings and to neutralise the powerful carrier groups covering such operations.
(b) To cover the vulnerable seaward flanks of the Soviet Army.
(c) To strike back at the West through its Achilles' heel, its seaborne trade.

German expertise, acquired at the surrender in 1945, was particularly valuable in two major directions. Firstly, in creating a large fleet of simple but reliable submarines which would meet requirement (c) and, partly that of (a). Secondly, in the development of stand-off weapons that could strike with minimum risk from the limits of an attack carrier's air cover, completing for the moment the requirements of (a).

By the late 1950s, the new fleet was taking shape, with cruiser-sized ships carrying the first 100-mile surface-to-surface missiles (SSM) and backed by new types of aircraft armed with long-ranged air-to-

7

Above:
Wearing a Dutch courtesy flag as she approaches Rotterdam, the *Inzhener Bashkirov* is typical of the many high-technology ships operated by the Soviets in numbers far in excess of trade requirements. A stern-loading RoRo, her military value in war is obvious; in peace she helps wage economic war by undercutting on the cross-trades. *Mike Lennon*

Below:
***Andaman* is one of 12 simple 'Petya II' class corvettes supplied to India by the Soviet Union. Besides demonstrating an independence of Western supply, India here acquired in the 1970s a class of escort well suited to her needs and within her capabilities to service.** *L & L van Ginderen*

surface missiles (ASM). From these earliest days, the problems of target identification and missile course correction at such ranges produced a need for co-operation between surface warships, submarines and aircraft, a mutual harmony that has been stressed ever since.

The growing submarine arm was supplemented by classic types of destroyer and cruiser in generous numbers to meet the demands of a *guerre de course*. Lastly there were numerous smaller flotilla ships, all with a capacity for minelaying, also meeting the demands of major roles (a) and (b). No carriers were possible with the then-available technology.

This measured and logical progression was interrupted by both East and West developing the submarine-launched ballistic missile (SLBM). Ranges of the first generation of such weapons were comparatively short, compelling their submarine carriers to approach the shores of their enemy fairly closely. Soviet interest, therefore, shifted to larger submarine construction, the ability to support its own ballistic missile boats (SSBN) and the means of countering those of the West. Anti-submarine warfare (ASW) thus took on a new importance, though with rather small and simple ships.

Succeeding generations of SLBM rapidly increased the range and area over which the Western SSBNs could be deployed. Soviet ASW ships had to go deep sea to counter the threat, and in doing so drew ever farther from the protection of their home based air umbrella. Armament was therefore developed along more balanced lines to confer better self defence, while dedicated escorts also began to appear.

Finally, improved technology provided for the introduction of hybrid aircraft carriers. Up to this point, it could be argued that the Russians had developed their fleet largely in response to the various stages of the perceived threat from the West. Having thus been obliged, however, to develop a new 'blue-water' outlook, the Soviet fleet, under the able direction of Admiral Gorshkov, has discovered for itself some of the other advantages of a world-wide presence, advantages which, though well understood by more traditional maritime powers, have been relinquished by them in various degrees since 1945. The carriers, though having a strong ASW bias to counter Western SSNs attempting to interdict Soviet SSBN sorties, have also a powerful offensive capability which is now supported by the new nuclear-powered battleships.

Russian naval power has therefore perceptibly

moved from a position of sufficiency to contain an attack on its shores to a new status whereby it has become a visible and effective instrument of state policy, a situation aided further by the constant quantitative run-down of Western naval forces. It can dispute any area of ocean vital to the interests of the West, it can support its own submarine operations and it can project power in amphibious operations of its own. It has acquired also a further and unique dimension in a large and technologically advanced merchant marine. The Soviet bloc is largely self-sufficient and requires little tonnage to sustain its needs. Nevertheless, it operates not only the more conventional merchantmen but also LASH, Seabee, large RoRo and many cruise liners.

In time of peace, this fleet earns vital foreign exchange, gathers intelligence and weakens current Western shipping pre-eminence by a vigorous undercutting of cargo rates. In the event of hostilities, the fleet would be a purpose-built auxiliary to the regular navy. Though the Soviet Union could lose the lot without losing a conventional war, by the same token it would also then be virtually unable to win it; the valuable auxiliary has also become an asset that needs defending, posing problems to the regular fleet that are akin to those in the West.

Characteristics of individual warships will be examined further in later chapters but this brief resumé will have illustrated how one state's fleet has developed by virtue of the continued stimulus of an exaggerated external threat. Once in being, however, a fleet does not stand idly about waiting for a war to occur. As has already been pointed out, it exists to project the policy of a state beyond the limits of its own shores and to safeguard its interests. Short of war, therefore, the fleet of Soviet Russia will have functions parallel to those of the navies of the West while at the same time each will have duties peculiar to itself.

Seapower is highly flexible and supremely mobile; there are few nations without frontiers upon which it can be brought to bear. As 'a soft voice backed by a big stick', its influence can vary from the subtle to the heavy-handed. Controlled foreign policy will use it as a sort of benign threat, although it could be argued that that policy will have failed the instant that a shot needs to be fired.

At its most innocuous, seapower is a visit to a foreign port to coincide with a national sales effort or, carrying a dignitary on a state mission, it will underscore his nation's commitment, demonstrating to the local population the importance it attaches to mutual interests. They should, in turn, be impressed by what should be an example of technological achievement and latent power. Ceremonial and the usual round of receptions are important for, competently handled, they will do credit to the flag worn by the ship and, through that, enhance the popular impression of the state that sent her. An example of such a visit was that by Bulganin and Krushchev to the United Kingdom in 1956 in the *Ordzhonikidze*, the first 'Sverdlov' class cruiser to be seen at close quarters in the West. A warship may also be the first source of organised assistance at the scene of a natural disaster, not only providing manpower, supplies and medical aid but even on occasion coupling her generators into a failed urban electrical system.

At what might be termed the next level of activity, a warship is used in the role of policeman. Fishery protection duties would formerly have been the most obvious example to cite; but recent years have seen a proliferation of declarations of national exclusive economic zones (EEZ). These declare sole interest in seabed exploitation out to, usually, a 200-mile limit. These may consist of tens, or even hundreds, of thousands of square miles of sea which may contain a considerable amount of international investment in the shape of offshore hardware such as drilling rigs and production platforms. Like the policeman on the beat, the patrol vessel is performing a token role of protection — a 'trip-wire' function. She has only limited power in herself but is in effect representative stating to would-be trespassers that 'to have your own way you will have to overwhelm me and, ultimately, through me, the state'. An example is afforded by the presence of HMS *Endurance* in the Falklands Dependencies in April 1982.

Policing such as this is performed by a state usually either in contiguous waters or in sea areas over which it has a legal right or responsibility. A rather more risky projection of the idea is the use of ships, usually auxiliaries with little or no armament, to patrol the territorial limits of sea areas bounding zones of political interest. Their purpose is the gathering of intelligence through electronic monitoring and their presence may provoke sharp reaction from the state being observed. Examples of this were the attack by Israel on the American ship *Liberty* during the 1967 war with Egypt and the capture by the North Koreans of the American *Pueblo* in 1968.

Allied to this activity is the use, particularly by the Soviet Union, of electronic intelligence vessels to observe and record procedures of warships on exercises. In this case the watchers may also have an auxiliary (and suicidal) purpose in what the American term 'Tattletailing' — the provision of continuously updated targeting information for first strike purposes.

More aggressively, warships may be used by a power to establish a continuing historic right of passage through a sensitive international waterway. This is undertaken regularly and completely legally by giving adequate notice of transit. A good example is the occasional passage of US warships through the Turkish straits into the Black Sea, which the Soviet

fleet would like to preserve as a private pond. That such activities can result in reaction was evidenced by the Corfu Channel incident in 1946, when two British destroyers were heavily damaged with great loss of life on an illegal Albanian minefield. As recently as

1981 American Sixth Fleet aircraft shot down two Libyan aircraft that were part of a force trying to dispute free use of the Gulf of Sidra.

A subtle but highly effective use of the warship is by transfer to emergent powers. Again the Soviets are masters of the art. Having built a vast number of SSM-armed fast attack craft, they possessed sufficient beyond their actual requirements to present them in batches to friendly and often unstable powers who coincidentally, but virtually without exception, have coasts flanking vital Western sea lanes. At a stroke the Russians threatened the routes by surrogate means, causing the West to devote more resources to the threat's neutralisation. They almost certainly obtained reciprocal anchorage and recreational rights for their own fleet. Finally they made the would-be

sea-power dependent upon them for technical back-up, which could then be politically regulated.

Moving up the scale of risk, warships can have a powerful effect by being interposed between warring factions, of whose dispute a third party state may disapprove. Risk has to be accepted that the warships of the third party may have to actively defend themselves or (probably worse in the political sense) be totally ignored. The third party must gauge the situation carefully before committing itself and make its move with a carefully calculated level of force. For instance, in 1922 several fleets, though predominantly that of the British, were present off the Turkish coast during the partial evacuation by Greece. A bloody conflict had developed and the foreign vessels, present ostensibly to protect the interests of their nationals, had a powerful catalytic effect in stabilising a deteriorating situation. More recently, units of the American Sixth Fleet physically hindered the operations of British and French aircraft carriers supporting the Suez adventure of 1956. No hostile action was taken but, by adopting this aggressive stance, the US government gave positive voice to its disapproval of the operation — disapproval which in the end caused its premature abandonment.

Closely related to this type of operation, though slightly more risky, is a friendly visit by warships of a third party to one of two other conflicting states. This represents an overt declaration of partiality, serving unwritten notice to the one side that further prosecution of the dispute would be unavailing as the third power would underwrite the interests of its protegé. This common ploy has been used in recent years by both the United States and the Soviet Union in locations from the Far East to the Mediterranean and Central America, although the current trend is for the superpowers to stay clear of conflicts not of their making.

Probably the last stage before actual hostilities is the sending of a squadron with an ultimatum. Again, the correct amount of force must be used to overawe without humiliation or the result will be a hardening of attitudes and the bluff called. Alternatively, it can be overdone, as in Mussolini's *opéra bouffe* bombardment and temporary occupation of Greek Corfu after an exaggerated incident in 1923.

What of the ships themselves? Whatever their type or function they see the light of day — in peacetime democracies at least — only after a lengthy degree of wrangling. Fixed and not-too-generous budgets inevitably stimulate the eternal debate of quality v quantity. No ship, no matter how good, can be in more than one place at a time. In fact, like the sailor's socks — of which he needs three pairs, one on, one spare and one in the wash — three ships are required to keep one guaranteed on station, the others being under refit or on passage. Even so, it is of little use constructing numbers if none can adequately fight or defend herself. Inevitably, the result is a compromise, sometimes successful, sometimes not.

The metal warship with an all-gun armament had a span of less than a century. Metal construction meant a great reduction in the likelihood of a vessel being sunk or destroyed by fire. At the same time that other

Top:
Seen here at Kiel, the Libyan 'Nanuchka' *Ain Mara* is a status symbol far too complex for the state's primitive infrastructure to efficiently maintain. It demonstrates friendship with the Soviets who, in turn, can use their know-how as a regulator while establishing a surrogate presence flanking the vital Mediterranean sea-routes. *L & L van Ginderen*

Above:
Showing the flag. Foreign visits, long a prerogative of the West's warships, are now undertaken other than to 'client countries' by older Soviet units. Here a large crowd waits patiently on the quarter-deck of the early 'Kashin' class destroyer *Krasnyi Krim* at Toulon. Alongside is the trials cruiser *Zhdanov*. *L & L van Ginderen*

Above:
**Routine docking reduces a ship's availability and is required
less often through the use of improved underwater paints such
as the self polishing co-polymers. The Soviet icebreaking fleet
is very much an auxiliary to the navy and here the 13,290-ton,
Wartsila-built *Leningrad* shows off her specialist lines to
advantage.** *L & L van Ginderen*

bogey of the wooden sailing warship, capture by
boarding, was virtually eliminated through the
introduction of steam propulsion, which gave more
power of manoeuvre. The need for a large gun that
could sink an opponent by hulling was obvious, but
advances in gun technology were quickly countered
by improved quality and disposition of armour. The
resultant struggle for superiority was a long one,
complicated by the arguments of a third lobby which
pointed out, logically, that armour was unnecessary if
one had the propulsive power to out-manoeuvre a
would-be assailant. An ideal in some quarters was to
produce a ship that could outgun anything that could
catch her, yet be able to out-run anything that could
sink her. In practice, however, most designs were a
compromise reflecting a balance of the three main
parameters — armament, protection or speed — any
of which could be enhanced only at the expense of the
others.

Speed demanded long, slim hulls packed with
boilers. Armament was extremely dense. For a given
displacement, therefore, protection often came a
poor third, being spread thinly between 'protective'
decks, vertical side belts and local thickening over

vitals. 'All-or-nothing' became the principle, a
gradual concentration of essentials toward an
armoured central citadel, leaving either end virtually
unprotected. By reducing the area to be armoured,
plate could obviously by thickened for the same
weight of metal. Improvements in the power-to-
weight ratio of machinery and the progression from
twin to triple or quadruple gun turrets assisted the
process.

World War 2 saw the heavy ironclad yield pride of
place to the aircraft carrier. The old order was further
shaken by the change from gun to missile and the
advent of the nuclear submarine. Bulky steam

machinery was edged out by the compact gas turbine. Improvements in stand-off weaponry put speed at a lower premium while rapidly spiralling unit costs collided with modest peacetime budgets to dictate the smallest hulls that would do the job. Proliferating suites of electronics for a multitude of functions, missiles together with their systems and stowage, and improvements in accommodation all add up to demands on space rather than useful deadweight capacity. Warships are now termed 'volume critical' as opposed to 'weight critical'. Beamy hulls support boxy superstructures devoid of protection and, worse, the diminishing weight of machinery below has been paralleled by an ever-increasing topside weight. Adequate stability is a growing problem for the designers and margins for added topweight are usually meagre.

Everything above the weather deck seems to compete for space. SSMs need blast zones, SAMs require two directors. Point defence SAMs have to be completely doubled-up and require clear firing arcs to give all-round effectiveness. The single remaining medium-calibre gun is pushed far forward to keep it clear of launchers and also to give it good arcs. After ends tend to be dominated by the stowage and flight facilities of one, or preferably, two helicopters, Gas turbines may be compact and demand little space below but their need to be changed regularly for servicing implies the provision of well-defined vertical paths for their removal. Large casings are required for the vast quantities of screened air necessary for their functioning and for the exhaust of equally vast amounts of extremely hot gases. A growing number of fixed and rotating antennae, serving a wide range of shipboard electronics, require careful siting to minimise mutual interference, to avoid slow incineration by funnel gases and to avoid jeopardising the nation's hopes of future generations of seamen through the effects of what is euphemistically termed 'Radhaz'.

CHAPTER 2

Armament

As the primary function of a warship is to act as a weapons platform, it is scarcely surprising that significant advances in weapon technology have resulted in major changes to the warship herself. Armament disposition is very much a function of armament capability and a brief look at some of the more fundamental shifts in practice over the years may be relevant.

Smooth-bore muzzle-loading cannon of the wooden sailing navy were of short range and liable to ballistic waywardness. They were mounted on simple carriages with little scope for training or elevation and indeed little incentive for it. It was an established precept that he could do little wrong who laid his ship alongside that of his enemy and it made sense to ship the largest number of the maximum size of cannon. The result was tier upon tier of gundecks, with two assailants pounding away broadside to broadside. If a result was achieved, it was usually by boarding and capture rather than by sinking.

Explosive shells began to replace solid shot by the end of the first half of the 19th Century. The battle of Sinope in 1853 demonstrated the devastating effect of these projectiles on fire-prone wooden ships and the antidote, ironcladding, was demonstrated equally effectively soon afterwards when floating French batteries with quite rudimentary protection not only survived the fire of Russian Crimean forts but actually defeated them.

Metal warships, once introduced, were heavier and could not be built as high, a single gun deck being the maximum consistent with stability. Rapid advances in gun technology were matched by those in specialised armour. Increasing accuracy and penetration at longer ranges had to be met by concentrating protection over vitals and the 'central citadel' concept resulted. This progressed to even greater concentration in the 'casemate' ships, which carried the smallest number of the heaviest guns on mountings which could be traversed to fire through any one of several apertures. A further advantage of this layout was a degree of axial fire unknown in broadside ships.

Barbettes, introduced around 1870, enabled one or two really heavy weapons to revolve over large arcs about the centreline of the ship and such a mounting at either end allowed a ship to manoeuvre freely during an action whilst still keeping guns bearing on

an enemy. It was then a small step to protect the barbette with a rotating turret and designers began to vie with one another to produce a layout that permitted the greatest number of guns to be brought to bear over the widest possible arcs of engagement. Superstructures were thus reduced to a minimum area and cross section. Again the quest for more guns resulted in more turrets and a dilution of protection, the direct result of which was the adoption of superimposed arrangements with each turret housing two, three or even four guns. Close grouping of armament and vitals was thus again realised and a minimum area of thick armour worked in, often on the 'all-or-nothing' principle, leaving the ends of the ship virtually unprotected.

Up to the end of World War 1 major fleets were still modelled on the ultimate aim of fighting a maritime Armageddon — a single cataclysmic action that would settle a war at sea once and for all. For this was developed the 'balanced fleet', where each well-defined class of ship had its own role to play in complementing the remainder. Despite the decreasing likelihood of such an encounter ever occurring, this style of fleet philosophy carried over to World War 2 which demonstrated conclusively the total obsolescence of some types and the unsuitability of others. Technology was replacing marine muscle and the need for more specialised ships was made apparent. Though the enemy retained the same general form in surface ships, submarines and aircraft, the potency of each advanced rapidly; the simple depth charge and various calibres of gun were no longer adequate, and gave way to a variety of missiles and other stand-off weapons. Each has had its own level of impact on ship design, generally in proportion to its range. Let us consider the major classes of weapon in turn.

The Surface-to-Surface Missile (SSM)

First generation SSMs were largely a Soviet affair. As has already been mentioned in the previous chapter, a priority with the Soviet fleet was to develop an ability to strike at a Western carrier force from beyond its air umbrella. To complement airborne stand-off weapons, therefore, a 130-mile SSM was evolved in the 1950s. It was a very bulky weapon, its size dictated by the power sources and control units of the

Top:
Conventional firepower still has relevance, particularly in shore support. Little altered since World War 2, the American heavy cruiser *St Paul* (CA-73) is seen off the Vietnamese coast in 1967 after having bombarded a power station some seven miles inland, a task impossible for any type of seaborne missile and which would, otherwise require a sizeable air strike. Note the added ECM pods and the TACAN beacon.

Above:
Hopes of updating a gun-armed war-built US fleet into an all-missile force in the 1960s proved technically feasible but uneconomic, it being cheaper to build specialist ships from scratch. *Columbus* (CG-12) was one of a trio of spectacular heavy cruiser conversions with two Talos and two Tartar systems for long and medium ranged AAW. No guns were provided initially but two open-mounted 5in weapons added subsequently can be seen in tubs. Note also ASROC and AS torpedo tubes.

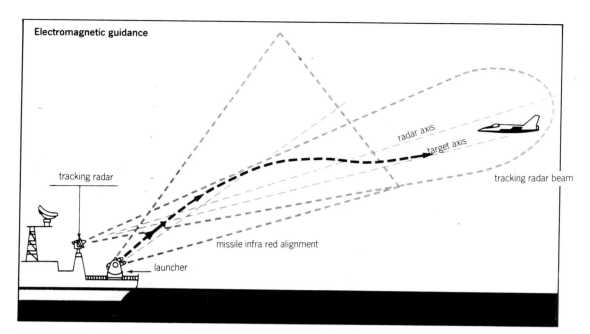

Electromagnetic guidance

tracking radar

radar axis

target axis

tracking radar beam

missile infra red alignment

launcher

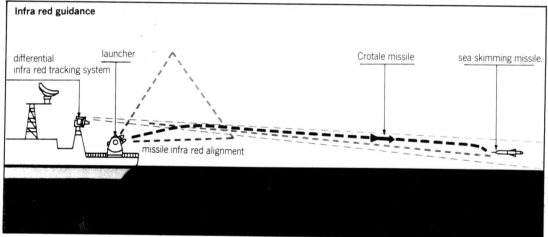

Infra red guidance

differential infra red tracking system

launcher

Crotale missile

sea skimming missile.

missile infra red alignment

time, a large quantity of fuel and a warhead large enough to cause significant damage to a carrier-sized target. Accommodation of two of these systems would probably have best been in a modified 'Sverdlov' hull, but the Soviets evidently considered a smaller ship to be less vulnerable. The purpose-built 5,000-ton destroyer-type 'Krupnys' were, as a result, completely dominated by their systems — they were ship killers, virtually devoid of any means of self protection. They were interesting first in their abandonment of the 'balanced' armament then the norm and for the daring departure of putting the magazines for about 16 missiles above the weather deck (there was, in fact, no where else to site them).

Though they were the world's first practical SSM

Above:
In contrast to the compact Crotale is the modular version, which separates launcher and director to ease installation on smaller ships which can thus use the director also to lay the gun armament. The diagrams show alternative modes of guidance. A reaction time of only 4.5 seconds is claimed with ranges of 1300m against helicopters and 8000 against SSMs. *Thomson-CSF*

Right:
The introduction of the Lynx helicopter has given frigates the capacity to strike at long range and in very poor weather conditions at surface targets, and the menace of the FAC in particular, with the sea-skimming Sea Skua missile, here seen hugging the waves. That the weapon will sink or disable a corvette-sized ship was demonstrated in the South Atlantic in 1982. *British Aerospace Dynamics*

Left:
Light automatic weapons, properly directed, remain an essential part of a warship's AA defences. Old pattern 40mm weapons of Italian origin are here seen on the veteran German frigate *Karlsruhe* together with their Hollandse Signaalapparaten M45 director. *L & L van Ginderen*

Below:
Unsophisticated by today's standards, the Soviet 'Krupny' class dated from 1957 but carried the first SSMs large enough to challenge an American attack carrier from the limits of her aerial umbrella. Outdated, the three-ton SS-N-1 Scrubber missiles have since been removed and the ships revamped for AAW. In her original guise, a 'Krupny' is seen here in 1971 cruising off Hawaii in the endless game of provocation played by both major sea powers.

ships, the 'Krupnys' would have proved unsuccessful in a shooting war. Even realising their full 130-mile range, they would still have been well within a carrier's lethal radius and would have been detected and sunk before an initial firing. Furthermore, detection and identification of their quarry at a range of 130 miles would have involved a third party — an aircraft or submarine perhaps (Gorshkov has consistently underlined the importance of co-operation between various arms of the fleet) which would have had to remain to give the missile mid-course correction when it passed beyond the

horizon and thus the radar control of the launching ship.

Typical of first-generation vessels, their short-comings revealed the real areas for improvement: a reduction in over-specialisation to allow a measure of self-defence, an organic helicopter to allow the ship to undertake its own targeting and, lastly, a longer-ranged SSM. Subsequent classes achieved these aims but only at the expense of increased size.

Compared with the problems involved in designing a successful surface-to-air missile (SAM), those of the SSM appear, superficially at least, to be simpler. A ship is large and slow-moving in comparison with an aircraft target and it is less difficult to predict an area in which to deliver a missile, close enough for it to acquire the target itself and lock on. Positive identification is a difficulty already mentioned, together with an inability to distinguish a chosen target from among a group. For a fleet that can operate with the knowledge that any detected 'blip' cannot be friendly, and is not too fussy in determining beyond doubt that it is hostile rather than neutral, 'fire and forget' SSMs are a simple reality. On-board electronics are minimal and the weapon itself can be shipped in a canister/launcher.To the Soviets again goes the credit for the missile-armed FAC as, alongside the SS-N-1 that went into the 'Krupnys' from 1958, they developed the slightly smaller SS-N-2 (better known as the 'Styx') which was paired in each of a massive programme of 'Komar' boats from 1959 to 1961 followed by an equally ambitious series of 'Osa' class craft, which each mounted four. Even though these craft were transferred liberally among client states of the USSR, it seemed to cause little concern in the ranks of Western fleets until the fateful day in 1967 when the Egyptians demolished the Israeli destroyer *Eilat* with two 'Styx' fired from within Alexandria harbour. The potential of the SSM was suddenly thrust upon the West and urgent programmes were put in hand to provide a means of countering these 25-mile weapons, which could outrange any gun, and to get a similar weapon afloat. Almost incredibly, the only available SSM was the MM38 version of the Exocet, which Aerospatiale had had the foresight to develop. Exocet, while having about the same range as the 'Styx', had the advantage of following a decade later — a true second-generation weapon of higher sophistication, less conspicuous in flight and more difficult to detect and counter.

In their canister/launchers MM38s are bulky and ships retrofitted with them have usually had to trade them for other armament. A decided drawback is the absence of reloads and it would be interesting to observe what tactics would evolve in a confrontation between similarly-armed ships, as could have occurred in the Falklands Conflict of 1982. Each round is precious and needs to be conserved yet at the same time salvoes are more likely to produce a hit through saturation of the target's defences.

The anxiety of a captain on this question of when to fire would be alleviated by the shipping of more rounds, this requirement in turn demanding a more compact missile. Such a weapon is the American Harpoon, which represents the third generation in being smaller and lighter than Exocet whilst nearly doubling the payload and range. Its compactness means that it can be a 'bolt-on' item, having minimal impact on available space. SSMs are not all large, the Israeli Gabriel and Norwegian Penguin being 3m to 4m in length yet carrying respectable warheads to a range of 15-20 miles. They were specifically for use by FACs which have become a potent force in recent years for the control of maritime choke points. The next stage in the evolution of the shipborne guided missile system will be in the general introduction of the Vertical Launch System — the complexities of a launcher, loading mechanism and magazine giving way to a multi-cell, underdeck system akin to a scaled-up milk crate. Each cell will be occupied by a missile, with its own silo and deck cover, the choice of mix depending upon the ship's mission.

The Surface-to-Air Missile (SAM)
The primary reasons why the West was apparently caught unawares by the rapid build-up of Soviet superiority in SSMs were firstly the postwar absence

Below:
The second-generation Soviet SSM was the SS-N-3 'Shaddock' credited with a range of better than 250 miles. 'Kynda' class light cruisers carry a quadruple launcher at either end, together with eight reloads within the superstructure. Having no organic helicopter, the ship would require mid-course correction from another platform to realise the weapon's full range.

Right:
A Sea Wolf point defence missile streaks from a six-barrelled launcher on a Type 22 frigate. This British Aerospace missile, here seen with its Marconi tracker, remains the West's best and combat-proven weapon for use against both aircraft and manoeuvring SSMs. A vertical-launch version, now under development, will allow retrofitting to extant ships with minimal disruption. *British Aerospace*

Below:
'Kyndas' were poorly equipped to defend themselves against the carriers that they were designed to attack. The following 'Kresta' therefore halved the number of SSMs carried and doubled the AA area defence systems. A helicopter was also added for identification and guidance purposes.

of any likely hostile surface fleet and secondly its preoccupation with a readily identifiable threat in the form of high performance aircraft armed with stand-off weapons. Concentration on the development of a suitable range of SAMs was therefore understandable.

American and British procedure differed in that the former endeavoured to produce systems that could be retrospectively fitted into the abundant cruiser and destroyer hulls only recently completed during the war while the latter decided to develop the system first and then design a ship around it. Both failed in fully meeting their targets. On the one hand the Americans produced satisfactory systems but the few retrofits undertaken proved that it was cheaper to build purpose-designed ships. On the other, the British were too indulgent in their control over system parameters, the resulting ships (the 'County' class)

emerging at approximately 50% over target displacement to accommodate a single Seaslug system.

Most of the first generation SAM systems were designed to meet a medium- or high-level aerial threat at about 15 to 25 miles range and were thus termed 'area defence' weapons. This type of missile needs to carry sufficient fuel for its flight and yet be sufficiently small to have the agility to out-manoeuvre a reluctant target. It is thus of too small a diameter to incorporate a fully active guidance system in its nose and needs the support of the launching ship over virtually its whole flight to guarantee a placement close enough to the target for it to locate it with its own sensors. This in turn demands the services of one of the ship's control radars and, as she is likely to carry only two of these, a co-ordinated attack by several widely-spread aircraft would be likely to prove fatal. In addition, the fitment of two shipboard systems will imply the requirement to house a large quantity of electronic equipment.

Early SAMs tended to favour the beam-riding method of target aquisition, requiring up to three separate radars. Firstly, a long-range surveillance set would identify a possible target, whereupon a second tracking set with a fine beam would be locked on, positively identifying it as hostile via an IFF (Identification, Friend or Foe) antenna and establishing range, course and speed. From this data a predicted intercept point could be computed; a further set then provided a fine beam of energy directed at this point and a missile was fired along it. This guidance beam could be shifted gently to take account of variations in target course and though it tended to lose its energy concentration at long ranges the missile by then should have been sufficiently close to acquire the target for itself. This could be achieved either by means of an IR seeker homing on to the hot jet exhaust, or by a semi-active radar homer. In the latter case, the energy of the reflections of pulses from the tracking radar would be used as a guide or a separate 'illuminating' radar would be employed. Only at this stage could the other radars be reassigned to meet other threats.

Though complex, the beam-riding technique is unlikely to alert the target to the threat until it is too late for it to take successful evasive action. To reduce the quantity of shipboard hardware, however, it has become more common to use semi-active guidance for the duration of the missile's flight. This entails a risk of the intended target detecting the radar, jamming it and launching decoys. Frequency agility can then be employed, the illuminator switching too rapidly between frequency bands acceptable to the missile's receiver for the target's countermeasures to analyse them and react accordingly. A drawback to long-range semi-active guidance is that the missile always has to point directly at the point from which the selected energy from the target is coming. Instead of flying a near-direct course to intercept the target, it follows a long curve, usually ending in a tail chase. It is apparent, therefore, that its range is effectively shortened. Again the missile needs to be in the final stages of its approach before the illuminator can be switched to a new target.

The third common method is command guidance, one radar tracking the target and a second the missile, to which instructions can be passed. Though not easy to jam, the system is best used over shorter ranges as energy dispersion at longer distances renders it difficult to compute offsets. Again, semi-active homing can be used to alleviate the problem but at the expense of shipboard complexity.

Recognition by the Americans of the saturation problem has resulted in the enormously expensive Aegis system. If one ship in a task group is fitted with Aegis, it can assess a large number of threats and, by

Below:
Modernisation and refit can improve short-term effectiveness at the cost of versatility. HMS *Phoebe* has exchanged her 4.5in guns for only four MM38 Exocets, with no reloads. A complex passive ESM rig at the masthead can presumably detect incoming emissions and double for the 'Huff-Duff' that it replaced. *Mike Lennon*

inter-ship data link, allocate the best ship to deal with
each and in what order. By means of time-sharing
techniques, Aegis can simultaneously control the
trajectories of several missiles to different targets.

Area defence SAMs tend to be large by virtue of
their necessary two-stage propulsion — a booster to
get the projectile up to speed and a sustainer to give it
range. Most stowages favour the vertical feed
method, with the arms of the launcher being aligned
vertically between each firing to accept further rounds
passed up through small deck hatches. To ease
demands on space in smaller hulls, the Americans
have lately adopted a dual-purpose launcher, firing
both AA and AS weapons. This is fed by rotating-ring
underdeck stowages and although it undoubtedly
saves space and can be fed in any order, it means that
two major systems are combined in one set of
hardware, a small fault in which can deprive the ship
of both. Less vulnerable will be the VLS, mentioned
above, where all rounds will be independent.

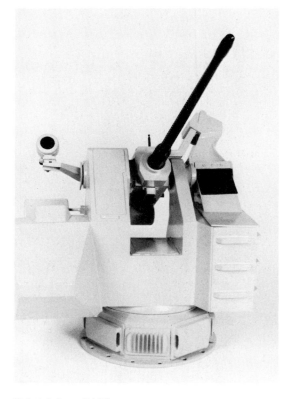

Point-defence SAMs

Theory suggested, and hard experience demonstrated, that area defence missile umbrellas could be penetrated by resolute and well-co-ordinated aircraft attack. To this hazard was added the SSM, either wave-hugging or terminally diving from the zenith to avoid radar detection. Meeting each of these threats at a safe range was, and remains, the function of the point-defence missile system (PDMS). Typical of the type and of varying vintages are the Soviet SA-N-4, the French Crotale, the American Sea Sparrow and the British Seawolf. First in the field, and still remarkably effective, was the British Seacat which retains its effectiveness because the PDMS is used primarily against targets approaching directly. Simple command guidance is adequate and ranges much in excess of about five miles are not required, so individual rounds are small and usually hand-loaded.

A successful point defence missile system depends upon good electronics to detect and confirm a threat, slew the director and launcher and fire automatically. Seconds are vital and for full effectiveness the PDMS needs to be an integrated part of a defensive system also comprising guns, decoy measures and electronic countermeasures.

The close-in aerial danger is posed not only to larger vessels of course; smaller ships, often of high value, are equally at risk and much effort is currently being applied to the production of a lightweight missile and launcher. One which shows promise is the so-called RAM or rolling airframe missile — a simple non-stabilised weapon loaded into a 24-cell container/launcher and small enough for the West Germans to mount one on the after end of their FACs and one on either after corner of the hangar roof of their frigates.

Medium-calibre guns

Though widely viewed as obsolete on the advent of the missile era, the gun has shown that it still has a vital part to play at sea. It is not a substitute for the

Left:
A Standard MR missile streaks into the air from the forward launcher of the American nuclear-propelled cruiser *California* **(CGN-36). Despite the imposing array of missile and associated electronics now deployed at sea, it has yet to be fully proved under extended combat conditions that they will be equal to what will be demanded of them.**

Below:
The first Aegis cruiser *Ticonderoga* **(CG-47) launches a standard MR Missile. Note how the extra displacement on a basic 'Spruance'-type hull has required the addition of a forward bulwark to gain freeboard.**
Aegis Shipbuilding Program, Naval Sea Systems Command, US Department of the Navy

missile but complementary to it; each has its own distinct role. A gun can be used against a 'soft' surface target that does not warrant an expensive SSM. It can be aimed-off as a warning where a missile cannot. It can be used against shore targets in direct or indirect fire; an SSM has little discrimination in the first and is useless in the second. A gun can pick out a designated target from among a group or against a landmass and its projectile cannot be jammed or decoyed. Finally, its ammunition is comparatively cheap can be stowed in reasonable quantity.

Having been something of a 'Cinderella' for some years, however, the medium-calibre gun has been usually cut to only one in number and that set well forward, out of the way. Here, it is subject to pronounced ship movement and wetness. The weight of the installation so far forward and the fine sections below are a temptation to designers to opt for smaller calibre. Far too many have specified the Oto Melara 76mm weapon; though compact, reliable and with a

good rate of fire it does not have sufficient stopping power to be of much use against a surface target, while its projectile its oversize for anti-aircraft use. Fortunately British designers have had the sense to keep to the well-tried 4.5in calibre — except in a few cases, notably the emasculated Type 22's, the Batch 3 versions of which will have the omission rectified, though only at the expense of being 'stretched'. American practice has been to retain the traditional 5in calibre, though the weed-like 76mm has rooted in the 'Perry' class fast frigates. The US Navy, indeed, has only recently developed a successful lightweight 8in gun for retro-fitting into larger ships, only to see the project wither for lack of funds.

An attraction to the use of larger calibres is the recent development of rocket-assisted fin-stabilised projectiles armed with a laser-seeking head. The target can be illuminated with a coded laser to prevent jamming — which itself can be sited remote from the ship. All the ship needs to do is fire the

Left and below:
Any ship proceeding into a zone threatened by air attack can be quickly protected by such weapons as the Short Javelin. With a range of over 4km it can be operated by one man and, being radio controlled via a stabilised optical sight, is more effective than heat-seekers against attacking head-on targets, which have a small IR signature. Trials are seen on HMS *Phoebe*, whose towed array equipment is also well shown.
Both Royal Marines via Shorts, Belfast

Right:
Point defence systems are vital to protect a warship against short-range aerial attack. It will be noticed how each round of the compact Crotale is loaded complete with its canister. A command-guided weapon, its axial guidance dish and television camera can also be seen.
L & L van Ginderen

round into the 'basket' of laser energy reflected by the target and it will home on to the strongest signal. With laser beams commonly a few milliradians wide, the guidance can be highly accurate. American rounds are available down to 5in and the French are developing a laser-guided 100mm projectile.

Close-in-defence systems (CIWS)

Often termed 'last-ditch' weapons, the CIWS are just that, automatic guns with a high rate of fire designed to stop the aircraft or missile that has penetrated the outer rings of a defence. Gatling-style guns have been developed by the Soviets and Americans, together with a Dutch/West German consortium. These weapons have a phenomenal rate of fire by virtue of a multi-barrelled assembly moving around a common feed. They are at their best on targets approaching head-on, where their integral radars will track both target and projectile stream and bring them together. Calibres tend to be rather small for effective destruction of hardened missiles, but greater inertia is sometimes incorporated by the use of depleted uranium penetrators of very high density.

A lesson relearned in the South Atlantic in 1982 was the effectiveness of quite ordinary small-calibre automatic guns against low-flying aircraft. Token 20mm and 40mm weapons mounted earlier have therefore given way to later versions of the 20mm and the extremely effective twin 30mm. It is noteworthy that on the British Type 42s these have been sited in the waist in place of seaboats, thus demonstrating the severe competition for topside weight and space.

Torpedo tubes

Except as part of the armament of a submarine or FAC, the anti-surface ship torpedo does not appear to have a place in the inventory of current Western warships, probably because to approach within torpedo range would be to court disaster from an SSM. Those tubes that are carried are for AS homing torpedoes, commonly the triple-banked American Mk 32 or singles built into the hull. The short-ranged weapons that they fire are not without their critics, who point out that if the ship is close enough to a submarine to use them effectively, she would already have been sunk by a long-ranged heavyweight. Soviet warships, whose functions are very different from their Western counterparts, commonly mount banks of four or five long tubes of full 21in/533mm calibre, capable of loosing either a long range AS or ASV torpedo.

Shipboard AS hardware has varying degress of stand-off capability; as might be expected, demands on space and site are roughly in line with potency. At the lower end of the scale, the AS mortar tends to be mounted forward for obvious reasons, even though it can be trained. Almost every Soviet ship has its MBUs and the Bofors 376mm weapon is common in the West. They fire a salvo of bombs with timing and trajectories set to create a three-dimensional pattern about the estimated position of a submerged target. The French pattern can be used for limited-range shore bombardment. Most swing into a vertical plane for rapid reloading. Few British ships now carry the excellent Limbo, even though such a weapon can

Above:
Except on smaller ships designed to a tight specification, the US navy has sensibly remained faithful to the 5in gun, whose 54-calibre version is seen here on the veteran destroyer *Edson*. It is capable of a firing rate of 34 rounds per minute and is currently the smallest weapon able to fire 'smart' ammunition.
L & van Ginderen

Left:
Much controversy continues with regard to the ideal calibre for the modern naval gun. The 'super-rapid' OTO Melara can fire at a rate of 120 rounds per minute with the ability to switch within 5sec from the surface to the AA role, firing proximity-fused ammunition. It is installed widely on warships down to the size of FACs.
OTO Melara SpA

Right:
Seen here aboard the USS *King* (DLG-10) the Vulcan/Phalanx has been purchased by the Royal Navy as an interim weapon. Self-contained, with autonomous search and track radars, the weapon can fire at a rate of 3,000 rounds per minute. The calibre of the six-barrelled Gatling is only 20mm but fires rounds of high-density material.

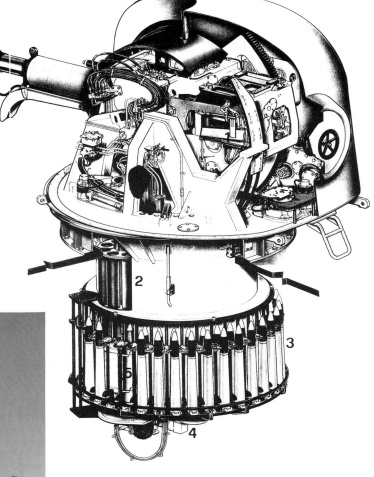

A cut-away illustration of the OTO 76/62 Super Rapid Gun Mounting, showing the feeding and loading system main components. (1) Rocking arms and loader drum, transferring the rounds from the screw feeder hoist to the elevating mass. (2) Screw feeder hoist, supply rounds to the rocking arms. (3) Revolving feed magazine, manually loaded and automatically supplying the screw feeder hoist with AA ammunition. (4) Presetting device to switch screw feeder hoist and revolving feed magazine for surface ammunition loading. (5) Surface ammunition loading station.

prove useful against a silent bottomed target, classified by sonar but virtually invisible to a homing torpedo.

Mortars were quickly abandoned by the US Navy in favour of the ASROC, whose rocket-propelled missile follows a ballistic trajectory to drop a torpedo or nuclear depth charge over a target at a distance of up to approximately six miles. Earlier eight-cell launchers and reload systems were demanding of space and current practice is to fire ASROC rounds as an alternative from SAM launchers.

At the top end are guided vehicles for carrying an AS torpedo. The Soviet SS-N-14 has full horizon range but, as this probably exceeds the capabilities of a ship's sonar a third party such as a helicopter is necessary to realise the full potential. The French Malafon is now elderly and of such a size as to severely restrict the number of rounds that can be carried. The Anglo-Australian Ikara is smaller and has a superior range, but where the Australians have retro-fitted the weapon into their frigates without too

much sacrifice, the British have sited it in place of the main armament of those 'Leanders' selected to carry it, the converted vessels now being helpless against surface attack.

There is no doubt that, nuclear weapons aside, the aircraft remains the warship's mortal foe. Whatever its prime function, a warship should be capable of meeting so universal an enemy with a reasonable chance of survival and it can be argued that a basic PDMS and CIWS should be a minimum fit. Should they detract from the ship's major role it is unfortunate but necessary as in the circumstances of war a vessel may necessarily be tasked for a purpose

other than that for which she was designed. Sufficient space and weight margin should also be available for updating; the American 'Spruance' remains a lone example of good practice in this respect.

Soviet warships have a high level of redundancy built in and are well able to defend themselves. American and British vessels all too often lack the range of necessary firepower, probably a legacy of the long offensive tradition where fighting spirit made up for material shortcomings. Unfortunately today's war is one of technology and courage alone will not down a missile unless it is complemented by the necessary hardware.

CHAPTER 3

Machinery

Unlike merchant ships which proceed for the greater part of their lives at constant speed, warships may spend long periods loitering or at low speeds, interspersed with spells of activity involving high power demand. In addition, they will be expected to have reserve power available for emergencies. They are required to have long endurance at cruising speed, to be able to increase from cruising to maximum speed quickly and to be able to start from cold at minimal notice.

With fewer ships available to a fleet, more sea-time is normal so the cost of bunker fuel is an important factor. In the decade to 1983, the costs of both distillate and residual fuels rose more than fivefold *in real terms* and, as the fuel bill can account for one tenth of the life cycle costs for the whole ship, an economic choice at the outset can pay dividends. Even more important is the need for machinery to be reliable and easily maintained, and capable of being run by a minimum number of skilled staff or even automatically.

The choice of plant available to the naval architect may at first sight seem bewildering — steam turbines, gas turbines, diesel or nuclear (alone or in combination), turbo-electric, diesel-electric, hydraulic or even exotica based on electrical super-conduction or magneto-hydrodynamics. Most need reduction gearing, some reversing gears. Multi-engine layouts need complex clutching. Some have orthodox propellers, some variable-pitch; some have unorthodox propellers, others no propellers at all. A few are fitted with auxiliary propulsion in addition.

Steam

For long, steam was synonymous with power. Even when alternative forms of engine were introduced, they could not match the steam turbine for reliability or sheer power. Now that realistic choices are available, however, steam's drawbacks are subjected to greater scrutiny. Steam plant is bulky. Turbines take dry steam from boilers at elevated temperatures and pressures, and expand it to do useful work in several stages. For the sake of efficiency, the turbine rotors revolve at extremely high speed, requiring several stages of gearing to reduce the output to a speed that can be applied to a propeller shaft. For

astern power, a separate stage or separate turbine is required. Exhausted steam is passed through a condenser to re-convert it to fresh water, wastage being made up from an evaporator, and the closed cycle completed by feeding the water back to the boiler. To reduce the size of individual compartments and the likelihood of crippling action damage, machinery and boiler spaces are separated. With larger ships this inevitably results in a two-funnel layout, the uptakes being a considerable distance apart. Frigate-sized ships, with lower installed power and with hull space in great demand, tend to feature concentrated machinery and single funnels.

By its very nature steam plant is part of the ship which is literally built around it. Though highly complex, it has been refined over the years and is exceedingly reliable; in comparison with other systems, it runs for long periods between major overhauls and is very durable. However, major maintenance is beyond the powers of the ship's staff and steamers spend long periods against a dockyard wall. This is wasteful, for use of the ship is lost to the fleet for perhaps 10% of its life.

Steam is labour-intensive. For instance, the crew strength of a British general-purpose 'Leander' is 260, while that of an equivalently-sized gas turbine — propelled Type 21 is only 175, a reduction of virtually one third. A further drawback is that, although boiler design has improved greatly, it still takes several hours to raise steam from cold and get underway. If rapid response is required for operational reasons or because of deteriorating weather conditions, steam will need to be kept on at least one boiler with consequent demands on both fuel and manpower. In similar circumstances, another ship with even auxiliary diesel or gas turbine propulsion could be away at short notice from cold. Since World War 2, the US Navy has increased pressures from a standard 600psi (about 40 bar) to 1,200psi (80 bar) to improve power-to-weight ratio. The plant has given more than its fair share of problems however, and probably accounts for the paying-off of the 'Forrest Shermans' from the first-line fleet.

Steam's one great advantage — that of burning cheaper residual fuels in boilers — has been largely negated in recent years by a move to standardise on diesel-quality distillates in the interests of logistics.

Above:
The British frigate HMS *Amazon* makes a brave sight at speed. Speed is, however, very expensive in terms of power and fuel costs. Type 21s such as these are fast by virtue of their COGOG machinery, their two Olympus engines, even when derated, producing some 56,000bhp. This is nearly double that available to the 'Leanders' of equivalent size. *Mike Lennon*

Left:
Funnel casings on all gas turbine ships tend to be bulky. As the picture shows, the insulated and muffled uptakes from two Olympus and two Tyne engines are of considerable diameter to pass the enormous flow of exhaust gas. The funnel is being lowered onto the Netherland's air defence frigate *Jacob van Heemskerck* during fitting-out. *Royal Schelde*

Ironically this is at a time when diesel manufacturers are making every effort to train their products to thrive on more inferior blends in the interests of economy.

Diesel

Except for the case of conventional submarine propulsion, neither the US nor the Royal Navy has shown any enthusiasm for diesels, despite odd abberations such as the 'Claud Jones' class on one side of the Atlantic and the Types 41 and 61 on the other. A truly vast range of diesels is available in standard production worldwide, covering all powers and configurations. Diesels are also economic but are unquestionably noisy in a world where to be quiet is to win. They are also highly responsive to the quality and regularity of maintenance, and an all-diesel frigate with four low-profile, medium-speed engines may well have between 40 and 50 cylinders.

Those all-diesel designs that exist tend to be small and of low power. For installed powers exceeding about 20,000shp it is more common to find diesels relegated to a cruising capacity, sharing common transmission with gas turbines. In this so-called CODOG configuration, the diesels offer approximately 25% of the power of the turbines, which are used for boost. Connected via clutches to common gearboxes, the prime movers are alternatives and not used together. The main reason for this is that the gearboxes would need to be far more complex to simultaneously accommodate two widely differing input speeds, and the resultant increase in shaft horsepower would not be sufficient to greatly affect maximum ship speed.

Above:
Seapower, American-style, still hinges on the self-sustaining fast carrier group. Though devastatingly effective during World War 2, its relevance and, indeed, survivability in the course of a modern conflict employing theatre nuclear weapons is being increasingly questioned by theorists. Here the conventionally-powered *Kitty Hawk* (CV-63) takes fuel and stores from the fast combat support ship *Sacramento* (AOE-1).

Top right:
To meet their required top speed, while retaining maximum flexibility and economy, most FACs adopt a four-diesel, four-shaft arrangement. Each engine here drives a fixed-pitch propeller via a reverse/reduction box. A refinement would be to adopt CP propellers, allowing the gearbox to be dispensed with, the propellers feathered and stopped in cruise conditions. CP propellers are not, however, easy to design for low cavitation at the speeds involved. *MTU, Friedrichshafen*

Centre right:
A popular layout in smaller frigates and corvettes is the CODAD. Here, each shaft is powered by one or two diesels, clutched-in as required to common gearboxes. As CP propellers are used, no reversing facility is provided and, for cruising, either shaft can be powered by one engine or one may be feathered, stopped and trailed. Resilient mountings may be doubled to minimise radiated noise levels.
MTU, Friedrichshafen

Right:
Though more economical than COGOG, the CODOG remains less common, largely because of ASW ships being very noise conscious. As can be seen with this layout for the new German F 122s however, modern diesels can be modularised like gas turbines and double-resiliently mounted to decouple vibratory noise from the hull.
MTU, Friedrichshafen

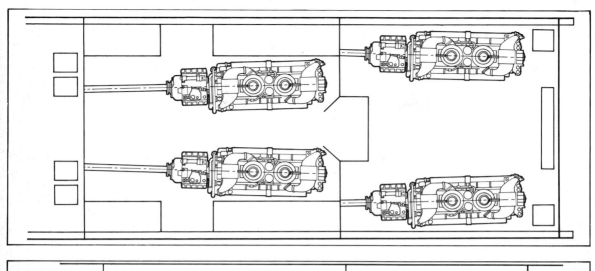

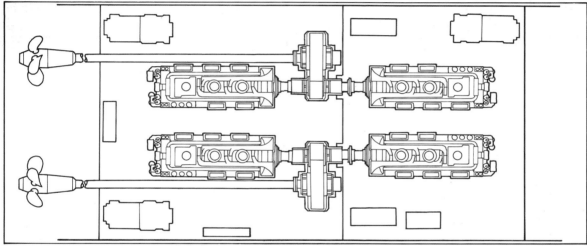

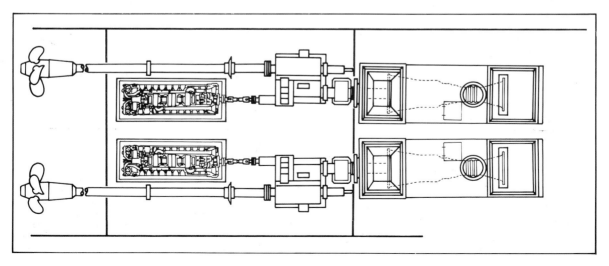

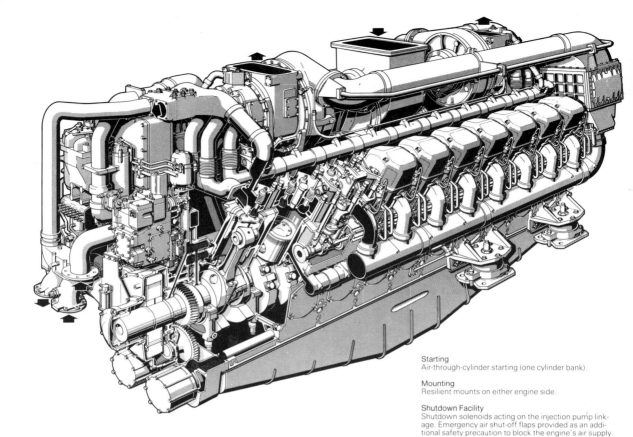

Starting
Air-through-cylinder starting (one cylinder bank).

Mounting
Resilient mounts on either engine side.

Shutdown Facility
Shutdown solenoids acting on the injection pump linkage. Emergency air shut-off flaps provided as an additional safety precaution to block the engine's air supply.

Above:
The cruise diesels of the F 122's CODOG propulsion system are MTU 20 V 956 units, a tally signifying 20-cylinder, V-form engines of the 956 series. Being of four-stroke operation, they cannot be reversed, one reason for adopting CP propellers. These compact exhaust-turbocharged engines, while complex, are self-contained 'bolt-on' items with a high power output of 245kW per cylinder. *MTU, Friedrichshafen*

Below:
West Germany has been particularly successful in recent years in the export submarine market. In a submarine machinery layout, the single shaft is driven directly by a double-armature motor with fine speed control. The motor takes power from four diesel-generator sets whose output can be directed as required to propulsion or battery charging. *MTU, Friedrichshafen*

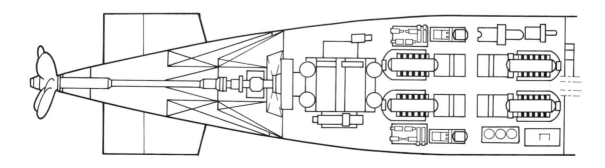

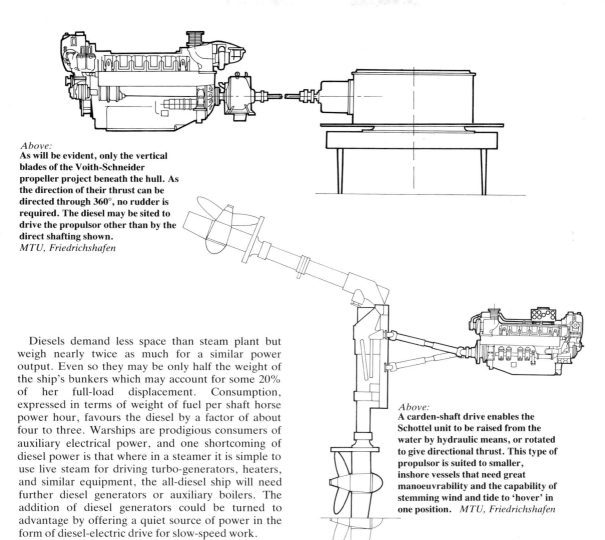

Above:
As will be evident, only the vertical blades of the Voith-Schneider propeller project beneath the hull. As the direction of their thrust can be directed through 360°, no rudder is required. The diesel may be sited to drive the propulsor other than by the direct shafting shown.
MTU, Friedrichshafen

Above:
A carden-shaft drive enables the Schottel unit to be raised from the water by hydraulic means, or rotated to give directional thrust. This type of propulsor is suited to smaller, inshore vessels that need great manoeuvrability and the capability of stemming wind and tide to 'hover' in one position. *MTU, Friedrichshafen*

Diesels demand less space than steam plant but weigh nearly twice as much for a similar power output. Even so they may be only half the weight of the ship's bunkers which may account for some 20% of her full-load displacement. Consumption, expressed in terms of weight of fuel per shaft horse power hour, favours the diesel by a factor of about four to three. Warships are prodigious consumers of auxiliary electrical power, and one shortcoming of diesel power is that where in a steamer it is simple to use live steam for driving turbo-generators, heaters, and similar equipment, the all-diesel ship will need further diesel generators or auxiliary boilers. The addition of diesel generators could be turned to advantage by offering a quiet source of power in the form of diesel-electric drive for slow-speed work.

Over the last decade, the SSM-armed fast attack craft has developed into a very potent warship and diesel drives of up to 18,00bhp on four shafts are virtually universal. Gas turbines have gained hardly a foothold in the market because of the limitation in choice.

Gas Turbine

Though not the recent innovation that it may seem (the Royal Navy was experimenting with small GTs soon after World War 2), the gas turbine at last looks to become virtually univeral in faster warships in the next decade. Where steam was very much part of the ship, the GT is built into a modular frame, runs a specified number of hours in service and is then exchanged to be refitted. It is so compact that complete spare units can be carried aboard and if necessary changed by a competent staff without dockyard assistance. Like a diesel, the GT scores by being complete in itself. It is very much lighter and less bulky than a diesel of similar power but loses out in being a prodigious consumer of air. The required downtakes, uptakes and removal paths have a great influence on the ship's layout.

Ingested air is filtered of salt spray, compressed and mixed with burning fuel, forming gas almost explosively at temperatures more than half as hot again as superheated steam. This gas is then blasted through a turbine in order to expand. A drawback is that the vast quantities of exhaust gas are extremely hot and, where it would be attractive to extract this heat for auxiliary generation purposes, it is not completely practicable. The generously-proportioned funnels are thus fashioned in a variety of usually ungracious ways to throw the hot exhaust gases clear

Left:
Steam from nuclear power provides the muscle for the catapults on the *Enterprise* (CVN-65). The complex nature of the FIA-18 is demonstrated by the prime contractor, McDonnell Douglas, sub-contracting to Northrop the centre and after fuselage sections, stabilisers and all associated sub-systems. *Northrop Corporation*

Above:
The US Navy's only attempt at a cheap, diesel escort were the four 'Claud Jones' class of 1959-60. Though having only one shaft, the ships had four diesels for flexibility and these were spaced widely, thus requiring two stacks. They were little more than an experiment and all were sold to Indonesia in 1973-74. The USS *McMorris* (DE-1036) seen here off Hawaii in 1969, became the *Ngurah Rai*.

of the ship's tophamper to avoid its early demise through corrosive cooking. Such heat loss is not only uneconomic but positively dangerous in a warship, allowing her to be easily detected by passive means and providing a useful target for a missile with an IR-seeking head.

Gas turbines can be run up from cold at very short notice so getting under way or cracking on speed becomes a simple matter. They lend themselves readily to automated control, thus reducing crew strength — a very important parameter in ship design and costing. Modern data logging allows the engines and transmission to be automatically and continuously monitored; deviation in reading from specified norms at any critical point triggers an alarm to initiate remedial action. Like steam turbines, GTs cannot be reversed and astern power must be produced using either reversing gearboxes or controllable-pitch propellers. Unlike the British and Soviet fleets, few other Navies adopted the GT readily for reasons of conservatism or lack of available choice. The Soviet 'Kashin' class destroyers — the world's first warships powered solely by gas turbines — are credited with having a power output of 96,000shp on two shafts; for a late 1950s design this would be highly creditable on only four units and they may well have as many as eight. Low-power first-generation British GTs are still operational in the remaining 'County' and Type 81 classes. Both are COSAG-configured, with the GTs developing the smaller part of the power and being used to boost the output of the steam plant when required.

Currently, the Western GT market is dominated by American and British companies. Rolls-Royce have successively uprated the Olympus to 21,000kW (about 28,000hp) in the current TM 3B model, and the Tyne to 4,000kW (5,350hp) in the RM1C. Due to this great disparity in powers and the poor efficiency of the GT when operated at other than its design power, the COGOG arrangement has become popular with each of two shafts driven by a gearbox into which can be clutched either a Tyne for cruising or an Olympus for high speed operations. After years of development the Spey SM1A is in service, offering a power of 14,000kW (18,800hp) and slotting nicely between the other two.

The current American engines are the General Electric LM2500, rated at a little less than that of the Olympus and the Pratt & Whitney FT4, roughly equivalent to the Spey. Newly introduced is the LM 500, to parallel the Tyne.

Nuclear

Nuclear plant is bulky and heavy comprising as it does a complete conventional steam plant downstream from the reactor(s). In surface warships it is further encumbered with comprehensive primary radiation shielding and heavy secondary structural protection to safeguard against the effects of a major collision or action damage. In terms of weight per unit of power developed, the nuclear propulsion plant for smaller warships is always heavier than a conventional arrangement of similar power. Only at ratings of above about 27,000kW (36,000hp) per shaft is there any advantage.

Submarines by their very nature can have reduced structural protection and gain so much in the operational sense that nuclear power has provided a revolution in underwater warfare. High speed combined with a hull form optimised for submerged performance has produced a truly formidable weapon whose endurance is governed only by that of the crew that mans it.

Nuclear surface warships were long the prerogative of the Americans, and only recently joined by the Soviets, who themselves had acquired vast experience in nuclear-powered icebreakers. Surface ships, even if nuclear-powered, can still be limited by their various other needs (aviation fuel, dry stores, ordnance etc) and the refuelling requirements of conventionally-powered escorts, so regular replenishment at sea remains a necessity. With the ever-increasing cost and scarcity of fossil fuels, nuclear plant will become more common, despite the current widespread popular hostility towards it. Whereas its adoption in merchant ships is a risky venture, and its large capital cost is unlikely to be defrayed over cyclic trading patterns, operational demands make it much more attractive in warships.

In a nuclear attack submarine, space devoted to propulsion machinery will be between 40% and 50% of the hull's volume. The very heavy reactor assembly will be somewhere just abaft of amidships, heating water in the pressurised primary heater circuit. Water flows in a closed path in this circuit, via a heat exchanger/boiler unit that raises steam in a secondary circuit. This steam activates the turbines of a conventional propulsion plant and turbo-generators, being then put through a condenser before being recycled via the boiler.

Diesel-electric

Something of a rarity in warship propulsion, diesel-electric systems were last produced in quantity to meet the requirements of the American destroyer-escort programme of World War 2 and in this case was to rectify the shortfall in the production of steam turbines and large reduction gears. Elsewhere, they are found primarily in special-service merchant ships, such as ice-breakers and cable-layers, that need particularly fine control and in the former case the ability to absorb violently fluctuating power demands without damage. Initial costs of diesel-electric plant are high and the system is on the heavy side. Its advantages lie in that the shafts are directly driven by DC motors which, appropriately wound, have an excellent speed/torque relationship. They are capable of fine speed control, dispensing with the expense, weight and noise of reduction gears; they are inherently quiet and can be simply reversed. Being comparatively compact, the motors can be housed well aft, if it suits the designer, thus shortening the shaft length. Motive power stems from diesel-alternators in the conventional amidships position, from which the output is rectified and switched at any convenient point. Although in normal transit a diesel-electric frigate would be as noisy as any diesel-propelled vessel, she has the attractive bonus of being able to 'creep' extremely quietly (for instance, when conducting surveillance with a passive sonar) by powering the propulsion motors from the auxiliary diesel alternators set higher in the ship where they are less subject to radiating vibrations through the hull. In an emergency even small service generators can be used as a 'get-you-home' aid. The projected Type 23 frigate for the Royal Navy will have four 1.3 MW diesel alternators for electrical power and long-range cruising; high-speed operation will require a pair of Spey gas turbines in a so-called CODLAG configuration. In the past, the Americans have been keen on the very similar turbo-electric drive, where they installed it in vessels as diverse as battleships and the war-emergency T2 tankers. It would appear to have little application at present.

6. Exotics

Super-conduction is a well-understood electrical principle into which much effort has been put to identify an application. If the field windings of a propulsion motor are cooled in a liquid helium cryostat, their resistance is reduced to the point where they can carry very large currents. This results in a powerful flux that greatly enhances the motor's output. Prototypes have worked well under highly controlled conditions, albeit with current density problems in the brush gear. The main drawback is the bulk and power demands of the cryogenics; indeed overall the whole arrangement seems to demonstrate similar figures for weight, space and output to a conventional diesel-electric system. The compact nature of the actual drive motor, however, would lend itself well to being installed as prime-mover within the confined space of the SWATH hull, if and when it is ever built.

A variation would be to apply electrical power to a cryogenic coil set around a duct running axially along the ship or set conformally into the sides of the hull.

Below:
Tracking the American carrier *Nimitz* in the Indian Ocean is a Soviet modified 'Kashin'. The world's first all-gas-turbine major warships, these formidable destroyers have a separately-directed SA-N-1 system at either end. Aft can be seen the tilted canister launchers of two of the four SS-N-2C anti-ship missiles, added more recently, together with two of the four 30mm Gatling-type CIWS with their Bass Tilt director.

Pulsing what becomes a vast electro-magnet sets up currents in the surrounding water and generates reactive forces that move the ship. Recent Japanese work has produced rosy forecasts of 10,000-tonne submarine craft moving at up to 100kts, but one can only speculate on the possible side effects of this level of power dissipation in the shape of, for instance, interference and radiation, heat and acoustic noise, to say nothing of the production of significant quantities of hydrogen and chlorine as a byproduct of seawater electrolysis! Research continues.

Water Jets
Aircraft propulsion 40 years ago moved efficiently from propeller to jet propulsion and the water jet may seem an equally logical successor to the marine propeller. Water is drawn up through a duct in the ship's hull, accelerated by passing through an impeller and expelled aft through a nozzle. For shallow-water craft the system has a great bonus in not requiring external shafts and propellers; even rudders can be dispensed with by directing the jet with a bucket-type deflector. The high-speed impeller, however, has all the problems of a conventional propeller while, more fundamentally, the principle is most efficient at higher speeds. A special case has been the hydrofoil-type attack craft which when foilborne has a keel-line well above the surface. The use of a marine propeller requires a tortuous drive through hinged link shafts that can retract along with their supporting foil struts.

A water jet exits neatly through the transom. As an example, the Boeing-built PHMs of the 'Pegasus' class have water jets driven by 1,800hp gas turbines, the same General Electric LM 2500s that power larger conventional warships.

Manoeuvring aids

Until comparatively recently, manoeuvring aids were rarely used in warship applications, but this is changing as their advantages are recognised in specialist fields.

The cycloidal propeller, virtually synonymous with Voith-Schneider, has been available for over 50 years yet is only now receiving attention for propulsion other than in tugs and ferries. Set into the underside of the hull it features a number of vertical pivoting blades set into a horizontal, revolving disc. As the disc rotates, the blades alter their incidence angles constantly under the action of a cam; this produces a thrust whose direction is variable with cam setting. Full thrust can, theoretically, be developed in any direction, thus obviating the need for rudders. If its reputation for noise can be overcome, it would prove ideal for MCMVs, which need to 'hover' for lengthy periods in tideways.

Another German invention, the Pleuger Active Rudder, incorporates an electrically-driven, ducted propeller in the rudder blade. As this will develop thrust along the line of the rudder at any angle the ship will experience a very powerful turning moment.

Azimuthal thrusters are assemblies incorporating drive and ducted propellers in a manner that allows both for their turning through 360° and their retraction into the hull. American 'Perry' class frigates, inheriting a reputation from earlier single-screw classes for poor manoeuvring characteristics have two such devices which also provide a 'get-you-home' capacity in the event of main propulsion failure. True side thrusters, set in transverse tunnels in the ship's hull, are not at present used in warships but find an application in special-service vessels. An example is Britain's new Seabed Operations Vessel (SOV) HMS *Challenger*, which combines three forward thrusters with two Voith-Schneiders. Good manoeuvring at high speed is built in at the design stage by patient experiment in the model basin to develop an optimum balance between inherent directional stability and rudder response. Mercantile practice includes specialist rudders such as the flapped Becker type and NPL's design with a roller in the leading edge (both of which can be set to angles greater than the conventional rudder's 35° without stalling) and the complex Schilling, whose paired blades are profiled and finned, and can work in concert or independently to produce highly directional thrust.

CHAPTER 4

Electronics

In the days of the sailing navy a warship could serve on some distant station, policing vast areas of the peacetime empire for months on end without contact with higher authority. Even in times of war the local Commander-in-Chief was rarely in faster contact with his government than that provided by despatch craft. The later years of the 19th Century saw a proliferation of under-sea telegraph cables being laid but use of these by warships entailed the risk of entering a suitably equipped port. Wireless telegraphy was introduced at about the turn of the century and was in wide use by 1914, but a ship's transmitting power was low and retransmission from shore stations was common for long-distance communication. Beside the advantages thus to be gained from centralised command there were obvious drawbacks — messages could be intercepted by an enemy and decoded, transmissions could be jammed and 'disinformation' transmitted to promote confusion. More seriously, however, the mere activation of a transmitter aboard ship could alert any eavesdropper to her presence: a simple loop aerial could quickly establish her bearing by strength of signal (direction-finding) and observations from two points establish her position. This technique was commonly used but never more effectively than in the anti-U-boat campaign of the World War 2. In short the radio transmitter, like all active electronic devices, acts as a beacon — a weakness that can be exploited by an enemy.

The upperworks of today's warships are dominated by a mass of antennae and electronics-dependent gear of various descriptions, falling into the following broad categories: Communications, Radars, Sonars, Electronic Support Measures (ESM), Electronic Counter and Counter-Countermeasurs (ECM and ECCM) and passive devices. The purpose of this chapter is to give a broad overview rather than a detailed catalogue of the many items involved. Like the tip of the proverbial iceberg, that visible topsides is of small compass compared with the supporting electronics below, designed to separate useful signals from the noise, to filter and process and analyse and display. Tactical data interchange systems enable ships to share information as it arrives and plots need to be computer-based to achieve the processing rates required to react to fast-changing threats. The electronics, their associated generating and cooling capacity, together with the highly-skilled operators make enormous demands on available space.

Currently, the 'state-of-the-art' outfit is probably Aegis, which necessitates a ship built around it, but evolution being what it is, full Aegis capability may well be incorporated into every hull in time. A precedent would be the dedicated aircraft-direction frigate of the 1950s, a type which never developed further as improvements in radars enabled her specialist talents to be acquired by many other warships.

There is bitter competition for prime sites aloft. Elevation, all-round 'vision' and a freedom from mutual interference are required and the best positions on what has usually to be a single mast or tower go to gear associated with the ship's major function and her survival. An additional complication is antenna-generated radiation hazard to personnel on deck and permanent screens may be found necessary. Antennae can be heavy and susceptible to vibration and have leads and waveguides that require screening and protection. For these reasons masts have progressed from simple poles, through braced tripods and lattice structures to today's plated tower. Besides being mechanically stiff, these give a degree of shielding against the blackout effects of an electromagnetic pulse following a nuclear explosion and the hail of fragments produced by the airburst of an anti-radiation missile.

Communications antennae are evident everywhere, for transmission and reception over a wide band of strengths and frequencies, inter-ship voice links and satellite communications. There is the familiar wire rope (single or in fans), there are whips (single, twinned or trussed), skeleton cages and cones, loops, dipoles, stubs and dishes. Linked with navigation are other whips for worldwide systems such as LORAN or OMEGA, loops with or without radomes and TACAN (Tactical Air Navigation) beacons in all-round arrays, often given pride of place at the mast-head and shrouded in a variety of 'beehives', pots or domes.

Most radar antennae rotate. Air search units tend to be large as the accuracy of the beams that they form and their range are functions of operating wave-lengths and thus dimensions. Two-dimensional

Left:
The 'mack' of the French destroyer *Duguay Trouin*, looking forward. The large elliptical antenna is that of the DRBV 26 air search radar while above it, facing aft, is the solid DRBV 51 surface/air surveillance antenna with its small IFF transponder on the upper edge. Pride of place on both masts goes to various ECM and ESM fixtures. *L & L van Ginderen*

approach, giving the pilot directly a continuous stream of information on his glide path and track.

Gunnery control radars may still be seen atop optical directors on older ships but various types of small dish are currently more evident. This shape of antenna will focus a pencil beam of energy to pinpoint a target with great accuracy and is, for this reason, of little use in general surveillance. Rapid-response close-in weapons systems (CIWS) are always in close physical proximity with their control radars, which are sometimes built into the same assembly.

SAM control systems have two associated antennae, one to track and/or illuminate the target, the other to track the missile. On older area defence systems these sets were very large, dominating the ship's layout while those for modern point defence systems may be small enough to mount on a single common pedestal. Early attempts at fixed arrays, the 'Scanfar' billboards in the American *Enterprise* and *Long Beach*, proved very expensive both to manufacture and to maintain and have been removed. The principle has been revived however, in both the Aegis ships and the 'Burke' class destroyers. Four antenna groups are built into the ship's superstructure, one to cover each quadrant. The energy beam is formed, focussed and rotated by the computer-controlled switching of banks of radiating elements, a total of 4,480 of which are built into each quadrant. Though effective, the system has a profound influence on the ship's topside layout.

As already noted, any actively radiating apparatus can be used to identify a ship's presence and, as many have distinctive radiating patterns, these, once recorded, can be use as a signature to help identify the type of ship itself. For this reason East and West dog each other's footsteps in the cause of electronic intelligence gathering (ELINT) and the seabed is strewn with strategically placed devices for recording anything and everything that will serve to label a ship. From patient collection and analysis over considerable periods, a threat library can be built up and issued to operational warships. In a risk zone the warship's ESM will be used to monitor all forms of signal activity, the data being continuously analysed for content and compared by computer with the threat library. Anything identified as dangerous results in various degrees of reaction, particularly bursts of energy in the very high GHz range.

sets have framed parabolic or planar arrays which form beams generally of narrow horizontal but wide vertical angles. Three-dimensional antennae are more complex, rotating in azimuth and simultaneously scanning vertically by electronic switching techniques. Surface search units are usually smaller, operating at higher frequencies to receive returns particularly from sharp edges and corners of the target — design features which are being increasingly avoided by naval architects.

Aircraft carriers require a variety of specialised radars to locate and guide down their aircraft in poor conditions. They may scan separately in azimuth and elevation, rotate at various rates or concentrate on a particular sector. Others respond to the aircraft's

Emanations of more than a second or so at these frequencies will more than likely be from a missile's homing system and speed of ship reaction is vital and therefore automatic. The detector will determine the quadrant and swing the point-defence director in its general direction. Any missile should then be acquired and tackled by either missile or gun ('hard-kill'). Simultaneously, alarms will be bringing the ship to full alert. ESM will be analysing the received signal and may then automatically jam it to confuse or retransmit it with a deliberate time shift in order to distort and divert ('soft kill'). Jamming itself is a rather crude tool, modern missile radars being able to overcome the problem by 'frequency agility' — switching frequencies rapidly and unpredictably. Furthermore, the jammer itself may be used as a target by an anti-radiation home-on-jam (HOJ) weapon.

A cheap solution to the threat may be sought in one of the many launchers that can eject clouds of chaff, or metallised foil, and hot infra-red (IR)-generating flares to confuse and divert the missile's seeker. Should a ship be optimally designed to present a poor radar profile, she could probably effectively tow a cheap (and expendable) radar-reflecting float as a decoy. Hot spots on the ship, particularly funnel casings, should be carefully designed to minimise IR radiation.

Should a ship be alert and well-enough equipped to detect and neutralise such incoming hardware it is probable that she will also have detected its launch platform for even if it were concealed below the radar

Below:
Fore and mainmast detail on the 'Spruance' class destroyer *Comte de Grasse*, the antennae showing the general purpose nature of the ships, which have no area defence SAM system. Prominent on the foremast are the bowl and dish of the Mk 86 fire control system. The mainmast's massive structure supports the SPS-40 search radar antenna, vertical tubular communications fittings and the beehive-shaped TACAN associated with the ship's LAMPS helicopters. Visible also are four of the ship's Harpoon launchers, adjacent to an ESM rig on a sponson. *L & L van Ginderen*

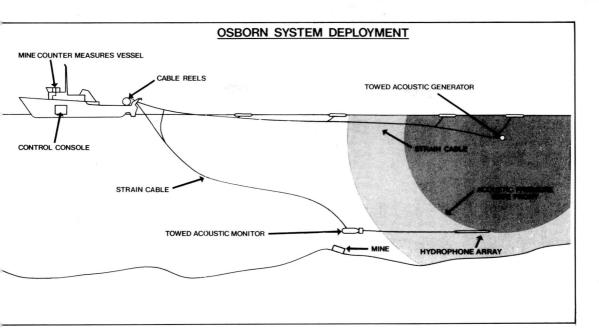

OSBORN SYSTEM DEPLOYMENT

MINE COUNTER MEASURES VESSEL

CABLE REELS

TOWED ACOUSTIC GENERATOR

CONTROL CONSOLE

STRAIN CABLE

STRAIN CABLE

TOWED ACOUSTIC MONITOR

MINE

HYDROPHONE ARRAY

Left:

Acoustic mines are dealt with by the Royal Navy with the Osborn sweep. This has two main components, the large drum of the Towed Acoustic Genertor (TAG) (*Left*) and the aircraft-shaped Towed Acoustic Monitor (TAM) (*Below left*). The former is streamed to buoyant strain cable and emits sound selectable over a wide frequency band. The TAM moves nearer the seabed, towing a hydrophone array, the signal from which is used to decide the exact output of the TAG and to guide the sweeper's movements.

British Aerospace Dynamics

Above:

Deployment of the Osborn acoustic minesweeping system which has been developed by British Aerospace and is in service as MSSA Mk1 with the Royal Navy in the latest class of mine countermeasures vessels. Osborn is designed to sweep acoustic mines and may also be used to counter combined influence mines when used in conjunction with a magnetic sweep. The system comprises a Towed Acoustic Generator, a Towed Acoustic Monitor, the necessary towing cables and floats, and an onboard control console. The system has been specially designed to withstand the levels of explosive shock likely to be experienced in operation.

ously emphasises and exercises this interdependence among attack platforms.

Only comparatively recently have submarines themselves acquired anti-surface ship conventional missiles. It has long been suspected that obsolete Soviet SSGs and SSGNs may well be tasked with saturating a task group with short range, low-yield nuclear warheads, probably targetted by a sacrificial 'tattletail', but the approach lacks flexibility in being pre-emptive rather than part of a graded response. Attack submarines of both East and West now have encapsulated anti-ship missiles which add a new dimension with the possibilities of 'pop-up' attack while the target's defences are occupied elsewhere. To offset the threat somewhat, the submarine will still need attack data prior to launch, particularly to address a specific target within a group and the more precise this data needs to be the more the submarine must lay itself open to detection and counter-attack. Once launched, of course, such a missile has created what is graphically termed a 'flaming datum' and the culprit submarine will need to rely on the confusion caused by an integrated assault to effect rapid disengagement.

The ESM antennae protecting a surface ship take a variety of forms. Groups of boxed loop antennae around the hull at deck edge level may cover the LF to HF band while VHF and UHF are monitored by array groups set at the masthead for all-round vision. Other systems may have small rotating antennae concealed within radomes, complemented by smaller, fixed aerials pointing skyward and set above fan-shaped skeleton frames known as ground planes. Many a masthead is adorned with groups of

horizon it will have had to positively identify its target and most likely have had to inject mid-course correction. If this intermediate agency was airborne, surface or sub-surface it would have represented a weak link in the attack chain — a link that could have been detected, identified and either neutralised or evaded before actual launch. For this reason satellites are being increasingly used. Soviet doctrine continu-

Left:
The effectiveness of the small warship is due largely to compact electronics, which enables it to operate effectively as part of a co-ordinated group while being able to control all its weapon systems from a common director. The Swedish navy is modernising its Proteus-engined 'Spica II' class FACs and the picture of *Pitea* shows that she has retained her six torpedoes while acquiring two RB15 SSMs in canisters right aft. Her 57mm gun is designed for the engagement of both surface and aerial targets. To cover this wide range of requirements, the craft are fitted with the Swedish Ericsson Sea Giraffe radar (*Inset*) system whose small radar rack is shown. It operates in the C band as a optimum for universal definition and clutter suppression.
Both Ericsson Systems AB

Above:
With no helicopter to dominate the after end, the Norwegian frigate *Narvik* packs an unusually heavy clout. Besides the after twin 3in mounting can be seen six indigenous Penguin SSMs and an octal Sea Sparrow point defence system, with its distinctive track and command antenna pair set on a tall pedestal. *L & L van Ginderen*

Below:
Nothing is too small to escape the attentions of the large Soviet fleet of electronic intelligence (ELINT) ships. Here, the *Khersones* doggedly pursues the British minesweeper *Alfriston* during the exercise Ocean Safari in 1981. Note the line of observers on the roof of the wheelhouse. *Mike Lennon*

An aircraft carrier is no better than its aircraft and the
quality of the latter's sensors are as vital as its own. Thus, the
radar of the F-14's fire control system is complemented by the
Northrop television camera system (*Top*). This can be used as
a passive sensor in low ambient light conditions or be slaved to
the radar (*Above*). It is particularly valuable in the rapid and
positive identification of targets. *Northrop Electro-
Mechanical Division.*

variously-dimensioned microwave horns, each sized to cover a specific frequency band. Soviet ships favour large, thimble-shaped domes set horizontally.

Today's encounters may occur at very high rates with responses entirely automatic, so it is vital to know who one's friends are, instantaneously and unambiguously, by means that can be neither easily jammed nor imitated. This is the world of Identification Friend or Foe (IFF) and another family of antennae. In peacetime or in low threat situations continuously-radiating beacons can be used but otherwise the platform carries a transponder which can be triggered by a friendly radar or a coded interrogation signal to transmit a brief coded response. Ships need to be particularly interested in identifying aircraft so IFF antennae are often sited on air search units, visible as a thin strip set upon their upper-edges.

Sonar, active at least, is to water what radar is to air but, as the short wavelengths used by radars are rapidly attenuated in water, sonar frequencies tend to be much lower, often in the audio range. Unlike the atmosphere, water can be uncomfortably shallow, can

have more pronounced thermal ducting and can vary in salinity — none of which will remain constant. Where radar energy will normally follow a line of sight, sonar energy can be badly distorted, scattered by bottom effects and bent by water pressure. It will be appreciated therefore that sonars themselves can vary greatly in their design to minimise the problems and can have a significant impact on the design of the ships that carry them. They can be small enough to be carried by a FAC (even commercial fishfinders and echo sounders are types of active sonar) or so large that specialist ships, eg the T-AGOS, are necessary for their deployment.

Many West European navies have a heavy bias towards working in continental shelf waters and have favoured higher frequency sets that can be made small enough for hull mounting. The containment is usually retractable but though this makes for cleaner hull lines at higher speeds, it also makes demands on the hull for the trunk and hoist gear. Current trends towards passive operation favour lower operating frequencies and arrays too large to be retracted. These are housed, in the manner long favoured by the US Navy, in a sizeable bulb at the forefoot. This fitting is flooded and made of sonically transparent material but is prone to make the ship slam in head seas. It is faired for optimum flow conditions but water-induced noise still demands that the ship runs at slow to moderate speed while listening. The sonar itself consists of a full ring of stave elements which can be switched electronically in the active mode to vary the bearing, elevation and width of the beam.

Input to a passive sonar is largely spurious — the tiny sound of a distant target, already distorted and attenuated by its passage through the water, being

Below:
Approaching 25 years of age, the Soviet 'Golf II' is now little more than a SALT bargaining piece. The construction is interesting in that, to avoid a large diameter hull, the designers have accommodated the upper half of the three SS-N-5 missiles within the long fin. The class is conventionally powered and the diesel exhaust smoke can be distinguished on the port quarter.

Left:

A port side close up of the island of the Soviet carrier *Kiev* shows the range and complexity of modern electronics. Fore and aft at the lowest level are the 'Owl Screech' directors for the ship's 76mm guns. Abaft the forward unit is a 'Pop Group' director for an SA-N-4 point defence missile launcher. Above the gun directors are the two bulkier 'Head Light' units associated with the SA-N-3 area air defence systems. The two massive rotating antennas atop the island are 'Top Sail' and 'Top Steer' for three-and-two-dimensional air and surface search. Pride of place is given to the spherical radome of the 'Top Knot' aircraft control radar. The four thimble-shaped radomes and the conical units above are ECM devices.

Below left:

Prominent on the after funnel of the American 'Adams' class destroyer *Richard Byrd* is the rectangular antenna of the SPS 52 three-dimensional search radar, providing target data for the single-arm Tartar launcher visible aft. Visible also abaft the funnel are the SPG-51 tracking and illuminating dishes for the same missiles.   *L & L van Ginderen*

Above right:

Later additions often make great demands on ships designed around other equipment. British 'Leander' class frigates, for instance, originally had a VDS well in the transom. This was later plated-in and some, such as the *Sirius*, now have the bulk of the towed array winding gear to add to the worries of the helicopter pilot. *L & L van Ginderen*

Right:

Down-the-throat view of a 'Krivak I', the Soviet's standard AS frigate. The quadruple SS-N-14 launcher is probably of a range sufficient to require targetting data from another platform, the 'Krivaks' not carrying helicopters. Various torpedoes may be launched from the long tubes visible forward of the seaboat. Two 12-barrelled AS rocket launchers, forward of the bridge, could be particularly useful against silent, bottomed targets in shallow water.

estimation of target bearing but accurate ranging will require a second 'fix'. Continuous signal processing on this scale requires large volumes of electronics, to which must be added the considerable generating capacity both to run them and to develop the energy for the sonar pulses when the mode is active.

Variable Depth Sonars (VDS) were introduced to overcome some of these drawbacks but have only limited appeal for shallow water use. They are very commonly fitted to Soviet ships which need to operate in extremely unfavourable surface environments. Being in essence small towed bodies, VDS can be streamed by a winch to a depth suitable to the conditions prevailing at the time. These conditions can be sampled both by surface ships and submarines through the use of expendable buoys. The data so gained gives the submarine guidance on the depth at which it can best escape detection, while giving the frigate in turn an idea of the submarine's likely behaviour and the best way to meet it through the planned deployment of sensors and weapons.

Towed arrays are really a variation on the VDS concept in being passive detectors that can be streamed at the end of literally kilometres of buoyant cable whose catenary will decide the operational depth. As the pickups are so far removed from the ship, they are little affected by it and can be deployed at useful speeds. Though many frigates are being retrofitted with towed arrays, the bulky winch and cable storage drums make severe demands on space.

largely swamped by self-generated and general marine noise. With active sonars the scatter produced by the bottom in shallow water creates a multiplicity of returns that can mask the one sought. In deeper waters however, the bottom can actually be used as a reflector for a steeply inclined energy beam where one directed at a shallower angle might well be deflected by an anomalous water layer. Returns need to be carefully processed, spurious content identified and discarded, and the remaining signal amplified and analysed. Passive sonars will need to be trained for an

The American T-AGOS ships are designed very much to commercial standards — their capacious trawler-type hulls ideal for the job. But they have no other function and are virtually unarmed, so once deployed on ocean barrier duties they need defending. Used in conjunction with SSNs and LAMPS III-equipped frigates they could be highly effective, particularly if they are capable of detecting an enemy submarine at the convergence zones — the areas where his noise is concentrated by being forced back to toward the surface by pressure effects. The first of these zones can be up to about 65km from the source.

At the other end of the scale is the minehunter's problem of identifying seabed objects in water shallow enough to guarantee the potency of influence mines. By cleaning up and mapping essential channels it is possible to simplify the situation by knowing the ground, so that any new object discovered by a sonar sweep can be investigated as suspicious. A minehunter's sonars thus need high definition but also the ability to do a wide-angle search to cover ground rapidly. They need to be able to 'look' sideways to define an object with sufficient accuracy to enable a decision to be taken to devote precious time to investigate further either with a remotely controlled

disposal device or the ship's divers. Sonars such as these again need much signal-processing support which has to compete for space with many other essential systems in a hull of very limited size; all of these need to be capable of withstanding very high shock levels from underwater explosions.

Like missiles, torpedoes can also be confused by decoys, and the ship carries such devices, together with their means of handling and towage. Once streamed, the decoy emits noise of a bandwidth and level that makes it more attractive to a torpedo than the ship itself. At the moment the system is largely self-contained and needs little electronic backup from the ship but as torpedoes are made more intelligent their active terminal homing is likely to become 'acoustically agile' and the defence will need to sample, analyse and retransmit with a fast response. This must involve yet more shipborne equipment.

Stealth — sensing without being sensed — is becoming essential for survival and alternative opto-electronic means of tracking and armament control are usually included in a ship's fit. Light enhancement by infra-red (IR) techniques enables a target to be viewed passively in conditions of darkness or haze, simply through the variation of its surface heat from that of its surroundings, although the old

fashioned concealments of rain squalls or heavy funnel smoke can still be effective. Laser range finding can be carried out remotely and is both hard to detect and extremely accurate. A television camera with good magnification and definition is another useful tool, again capable of entirely remote operation.

Finally, there are the means by which ships co-ordinate their activities with other platforms, whether surface, subsurface, aerial or ashore. Naval tactical data systems keep orderly the many threads that compose the complex tapestry of a maritime operation, receiving inputs from every available source, sifting it, and sharing it to maximise the effectiveness of each component platform. Each major fleet has its own system, the British ADAWS or CAAIS, the American NTDS, the Dutch SEWACO and the French SENITS being examples. Despite a great measure of compatibility between those used by NATO fleets the ideal must still be a commonly acceptible system. Processing and display inevitably demand much volume.

Electronics make modern sea warfare possible, influence greatly the ships carrying them and the tactics that they use. Though progress will result in continued improved capability and miniaturisation, this is true for both attacker and attacked, so space is still likely to be the main victim as each seeks advantage. Electronics may be the means of winning but can also be an Achilles' heel for counter-activity.

CHAPTER 5

Aviation

From the earliest years of aviation itself, ingenious men worked at the problem of operating aircraft, both lighter and heavier than air, from warships — for the purposes of offence, defence and observation. Where the French and Russians were early in the field, it was the Royal Navy that was to develop early pre-eminence under the stimulus of World War 1. Despite the fragile and primitive nature of available machines, the service used them in all possible roles. In defence, fighters rose precariously from sleds towed at high speeds by destroyers to counter the Zeppelin problem. Offensively, wheeled aircraft were employed in the world's first carrier strike against Zeppelin sheds at Tondern, while seaplanes from converted cross-channel packets staggered into the air from suitably calm Mediterranean waters to pester the grounded *Goeben* with toy bombs and then more ambitiously to sink the first ship by air-dropped torpedo. Converted merchantmen and warships used balloons extensively for spotting the fall of shot in bombardments. This was a luxury that depended upon local superiority and, when naval aircraft spotted successfully for the *Queen Elizabeth* shooting indirectly across the breadth of the Gallipoli peninsula, it was a significant step forward.

The many advantages conferred by an air arm were quite clearly demonstrated in the course of the war but development was inhibited by the inability of the ships to both launch and recover the higher performance (ie wheeled) aircraft. Before the war's end the British had again produced the ship for the job. A converted Italian liner to be sure, she nevertheless pioneered successfully the basic through-flightdeck-over hangar-over hull layout that remains valid for aircraft carriers today. Developed rapidly from 1918 to the early 1950s, the carrier became virtually the sole source of marine-based airpower for offence and defence; aircraft flew from other ships almost exclusively in the interests of reconnaissance and spotting.

World War 2 was to see the carrier come of age; but the British, as woefully unprepared as ever, needed to fall back on native ingenuity to produce stopgaps such as the MAC and CAM ships which prophetically foreshadowed the developments of today. Fleet carriers, however, emerged from the war as undisputed queens of the board and existed in such numbers as to inhibit further development and, indeed, the imagination of a naval world beyond their lifespans.

Even so, their potential was limited. Most had been designed at the end of the 1930s and rapid development in wartime aircraft had already cut the numbers stowed. Jet propulsion brought ever larger and heavier aircraft with poor low-speed characteristics that demanded powerful catapults, strengthened decks and larger elevators to operate them.

Even stretched in potential by the addition of necessarily disproportionate angled decks, the carriers' departures were only delayed. As more and more passed through obsolescence to the breakers there came the realisation that there was no way in which replacements could be made on anything like a one-for-one basis. Difficult for the Americans, it proved impossible for the British. A new direction was needed.

By this time a new element had appeared in the form of the helicopter. Though, in its earliest forms, it had been used by both German and American naval forces during World War 2, its miniscule payload had restricted it to short observation flights. By the first half of the 1950s, however, it had developed sufficiently to warrant examination of the possibilities of putting it aboard frigate-sized ships. The stimulus for this lay more in the introduction of the high speed submarine, and as the power most likely to suffer through attack from this quarter, the British were again predictably early in the field.

Once nuclear power had been married to the high-speed hull form, the submarine was well ahead of the ASW surface ship, which could no longer employ the weapons and techniques so effective only a decade earlier. No longer could the ship expect to outpace her quarry for, though still rather inferior in terms of speed, the latter had virtually indefinite endurance and was not subject to the inhibiting effects of wind and sea. Though the ship could detect the submarines at a range in excess of one mile, it had no means of attacking it and precious little chance of closing it. Working in quiet conditions below, submarine sonars were rapidly getting the edge over their ship-mounted equivalents, enabling the submarine increasingly to seek or decline action as it thought fit. As submarines had yet to emerge as the

best ASW platform, it became vital to give the surface escort a boost in potential. If a helicopter could be carried by a ship, it could function as a quick-reaction weapon or sensor carrier, working under the ship's control out to the practical limits of detection range. This would mean that a frigate would no longer have to run at higher speeds, being able to operate at that best suited to sonar conditions and possibly economising on fuel in the process. Targets could be located at greater ranges and, instead of losing sonar contact on increasing speed for an attack, the ship could vector her helicopter on to a sonar bearing to drop sonobouys in sufficient numbers to allow the ship to be guided in unobtrusively. Alternatively, the helicopter itself could carry the weapon, relying on the ship for data on the target's position. Either way, the proposal looked promising.

American opinion differed, favouring an armed drone AS helicopter (DASH) combined with a stand-off weapon aboard the ship in the shape of the AS rocket (ASROC). As a concept DASH was imaginative. With no pilot aboard, corners could be cut and risks accepted to reduce the size of the aircraft to a bare minimum. All its payload could thus be utilised for fuel and weaponry and the impact on the ship's layout would be minimised, a low-height hangar and small flight pad being comparatively easily

retro-fitted to the great numbers of increasingly obsolete destroyers of World War 2 vintage. Unfortunately DASH was ahead of the technology needed to control it for though the submerged target could be tracked on the sonar plot, the helicopter's progress needed to be monitored by radar and feeding these inputs on to a common display was not then feasible. Furthermore, although the machine could receive orders from its controller, it was unable to transmit any acknowledgement of either receipt or reaction. Neither plot nor feedback developed quickly enough to prevent the system falling victim to a crisis of confidence in the fleet, which was suffering a high failure rate. The project was abandoned, with many modernised destroyers doomed thereafter to carry undersized and useless hangars while boasting only the effective but, in itself, inadequate ASROC as their AS armoury, Strangely the Japanese, who relied primarily on US technology for their new fleet, also acquired DASH, stuck at it and made it work.

From the outset, the British took the view that a flight crew was fully justifiable penalty and, following successful trials from temporary pads at the after end of a pair of Type 15 frigates in the late 1950s, ordered the Type 81s ('Tribals') as the first frigates with organic helicopters. Oddly, the little Wasp that they carried had little impact on the ship's layout by virtue of incorporating an ingenious deckhouse hangar whose folding roof doubled as a flight pad. Despite the two funnels necessitated by the ship's COSAG machinery the flightpad was sited well forward, decreasing ship acceleration effects and improving dryness. The greatest visual impact was in the suppression of mainmast, the large antenna of the search radar being sited instead on a substantial foremast.

The drawback to the Wasp helicopter was its small payload; once the DASH programme had been aborted, the Americans opted (after a considerable time lapse) for something larger, possible because of their more generously dimensioned escorts. The advantage of a larger aircraft is its greater degree of autonomy, carrying not only weapons and sensors but also a data link to the ship. A suitable airframe existed in the Kaman-built UH-2A, which had entered US naval service as early as 1960 in the search-and-rescue role. Given a second engine and suitable modification it became the SH-2D/F Seasprite, the heart of the so-called LAMPS (Light Airborne Multi-purpose System) for which ship facilities had to be greatly extended in a programme commencing in 1972. The acronym LAMPS sums up the American viewpoint that the aircraft forms a whole system. Not endowed with great endurance, the SH-2 relies on the mother ship to designate the general search area, the target being pinpointed by dropping and interrogating sonobouys. Fifteen are carried, both active and passive, their outputs being relayed over the helicopter's data link in real time for processing aboard the ship.

A further detection aid carried is the Magnetic Anomaly Detector (MAD), which when streamed by the aircraft can sense the large mass of metal of a submerged submarine by the manner in which it distorts the earth's natural magnetic field. Currently, a submerged submarine has little chance of detecting a helicopter overhead as long as the latter has used passive devices in its search. The speed at which data can be exchanged and processed between aircraft and mother ship is crucial to a successful attack.

This capability has another application in over-the-horizon (OTH) targetting for the ship's Harpoon SSMs, now being fitted generally throughout the USN and which have been purchased by the Royal Navy. These missiles have a range of over 100km at which a surface target is usually invisible to the ship's radar by virtue of the earth's curvature. A suspected target must be positively identified before engagement is possible. It may be concealed in a zone of high traffic density, its own return unrecognised amid many others. It may deliberately be using a commercial radar, to be classified by ESM as non-combatant. It may return no IFF (Identification, Friend or Foe) signal but this may indicate no more than a friend with inoperable gear or a neutral. The helicopter can

Above left:
When in September 1980 HMS *Ark Royal* left Plymouth for the breakers, the Royal Navy lost the last of its fixed-wing attack carriers. At this point in its long history it degenerated from a first class force with world-wide capability into an essentially NATO fleet. Naval pre-eminence, once lost, has historically never been regained.

Right:
Even a 40 year-old carrier is better than no carrier at all. V/STOL has given back the small carrier its strike and defence component and the Spanish have wisely continued to run the elderly *Dedalo* until the new *Principe de Asturias* is completed. Eight of the ship's mixed helicopter complement and one Harrier/Matador are on deck. *L & L van Ginderen*

certify identity but may itself come under attack if the target is indeed unfriendly. It must therefore be burdened with passive equipment to avoid alerting a target; its radar will thus be supplemented by such items as light-enhanced optics on gyro-stabilised mounts (a helicopter is a vibration-prone platform) or infra-red gear. Even so detection may be inevitable and further active and passive devices must be carried for the aircraft's protection. Once identified, a target's positional co-ordinates and estimated course and speed can be transmitted to the ship which can launch SSMs against a computed intercept point. At such a range, however, flight time may well be 5min, enabling a target travelling at 30kt to have manoeuvred to be anywhere in a circle of some 6km in diameter. Though the missiles will have some form of terminal guidance they need to be put into a zone close enough to the target in range and bearing to allow the homing head to acquire it. It should be remembered that the missiles themselves will be following the wave profile, flying very low to avoid

detection themselves but making their own radar horizon very limited. Only when the helicopter has put the SSMs directly or indirectly into their acquisition zone can it disengage.

It was the Canadian Navy, ironically often criticised for being both undersized and obsolescent, that

produced a real step forward in the ASW ocean escort by putting not one but two helicopters aboard, and Sea Kings at that. The impact of their accommodation was such that the ship was wisely designed around them. The result was the 'Tribal' class DDHs which, on a hull of a size comparable with that of a British Type 22, have considerable AS potential. The hangar and flight pad for the two CHSS-2s are set well forward, giving the ships a high, boxy silhouette but leaving space aft for the bulk of a towed array. A Sea King's range is about 1,000km, compared with a Seasprite's 675km but, at take off, weighs over 8½ tonnes compared with only 5½. Decreasing ship motion improves the aircraft's operational envelope and the Canadians have incorporated flume stabilisers to reduce rolling, particularly at low speed. They have also fitted the Beartrap haul-down gear by which the helicopter, hovering steadily, is winched down on a constant-tension line to the moving deck, after which it is transferred by power along a track into its hangar — a hazardous procedure for unassisted muscle power in any sort of sea.

European fleets have not attempted to be as ambitious as the Canadian, primarily because they need a more general purpose weapons fit specification. Currently, the Anglo-French Lynx and the Italian Agusta-Bell 212 ASW are typical, but being smaller are still essentially weapons platforms dependent largely upon the qualities and limitations of a parent ship's sensors. A replacement for the former aircraft is being developed in the EH-101, a joint Anglo-Italian venture.

In the summer of 1984, the Americans commenced deployment of what should represent the current Western state-of-the-art — LAMPS III (LAMPS II never achieved operational status), based on the Sikorsky SH-60B Sea Hawk. It should do everything that a LAMPS I can, but better, with possibilities for general surveillance and (possibly a pious hope) early warning of incoming SSMs. Unfortunately, the Sea Hawk is as large as a Sea King, which has limited its application, and still lacks a suitable air-to-surface missile (ASM). Only the later FFG 7s, DD963 and follow-ons, CG 47s and possibly the new DDG 51s are slated to get LAMPS III, other classes having to soldier on with the earlier system. It is not only a ship's appearance that is dominated by the addition of a helicopter. For instance, two LAMPS III helicopters require a 21-man flight detachment comprising three 3-man flight crews and 12 men for

maintenance and handling. On a FFG-7 this represents about one eighth of the total crew strength. Trials with aircraft showed the frigates to be too short, so they had to be given a transom extension of 2.5m. Then found to be too lively as platforms, they were expensively fitted with active fin stabilisers.

An increasingly important bonus conferred by a modern helicopter is its ability to act autonomously with ASMs in support of the mother ship. The

Below:
Sea training; a Culdrose-based Sea King aboard the RFA *Engadine*. Though the ship is built along spacious mercantile lines, helicopters of this size are still a tight fit, evidenced particularly by the lashing down of two of the aircraft's five main rotor blades. *Westland Helicopters Ltd*

SSM-armed fast attack craft (FAC) operated by many fleets that would seek to control maritime choke points rarely operate singly and can target a ship out to horizon range. In return they make small, fleeting targets unsuitable for one of the ship's few SSM rounds, yet constituting a deadly threat that cannot be ignored, and which will probably be beyond the range of the single gun common to all too many frigates. For the ship to rely on detecting, seducing and destroying incoming SSMs is extremely hazardous and the only real cure is to destroy the source. Most FACs are still highly vulnerable to air attack and helicopter-borne combinations such as the British Sea Skua ASM and Sea Spray radar have been proved lethal.

The Soviet Navy came late to helicopters afloat. One reason is that in the Northern waters the 'window' in which they can operate is greatly limited. It was more appropriate to be able to locate and engage a target with the ship herself. Development was therefore concentrated on variable-depth sonars (VDS) and towed arrays to supplement the ship's hull-mounted sonars, which are more weather-dependent. A large number of Soviet hydrographic research ships have over the years amassed a vast fund of understanding of the vagaries of the ocean's acoustic properties enabling the development of AS missiles that can be targetted confidently out to the first convergence zone, some 60km distant.

In all probability, however, Soviet priorities were also different to those of NATO for of late helicopters have become more common, ASW ships carrying the Hormore A or the new Helix while ships of surface action groups (SAG) take the Hormore B for targetting purposes. So-called battlecruisers of the 'Kirov' type have a large waterplane hull with a broad after run that enables several helicopters, possibly as many as five, to be stowed in underdeck accommodation. Probably both types of aircraft are carried.

Helicopters working in groups are far more effective than on their own. Both the French and Italian fleets recognised this early and produced the 'Jeanne d'Arc' and 'Andrea Doria' types. The Japanese followed with roughly similar ships to the Italians but the British, in attempting to convert a pair of obsolescent 'Tiger' class cruisers, demonstrated only their total unsuitability for the task.

Amphibious warfare ships by their very nature have possibilities of large, unencumbered spaces topside and these are used by very large helicopters in both the assault and supply modes. The ships are unsuitable for operating helicopters for ASW purposes.

Task groups may be accompanied almost continuously by a large, multi-purpose supply ship. Her capacious hull may well be a useful place to garage and service the helicopters for the group; the Dutch 'Poolsters' are an example of this practice. The early form of the British Type 23 was slated to receive only a flight pad — the stowage and facilities for all the helicopters of the group being aboard a specially configured auxiliary. As warships rarely operate in idealised groups in time of war, the reasoning was specious and fortunately abandoned.

As it improves its performance and versatility the helicopter, like the aircraft, will inevitably increase its size and demands on the parent ship. Its impact can only increase and the ship will almost certainly need to be designed around it. As already noted, it was the ever-increasing size, weight and performance of aircraft that killed the 'classic' aircraft carrier.

With spiralling acquisition and running costs the Americans were reduced finally to a goal of 15 decks but regrettably the British Government made a post-Suez decision that carriers were too expensive a luxury. By withdrawing forces from 'East of Suez' it advanced the nonsensical corollary that attack carriers would therefore no longer be required and could be phased out without replacement. This was to conveniently ignore all other out-of-area responsibilities, and to suppose that sea power can rely on the umbrella of land-based air power. History has many examples to show that this is a fallacy, with results ranging from the disappointing to the totally disastrous.

The planned CVA 01 was, therefore, never built. This was probably because any one ship is rarely of use, due to being under refit or being wrongly placed. Three units are the prescribed minimum and these could not be afforded. Fortunately, within the Royal Navy men abounded who believed that maritime air power did not necessarily have to be reduced to the helicopter. In V/STOL they saw the way ahead and, against heavy odds, nursed through a troubled gestation the Through-Deck Cruiser, the first of which was HMS *Invincible*. The terminology was necessary because of the (then) political unacceptability of the category Aircraft Carrier although this silliness has now been dropped, the class being termed CVS or Anti-submarine Carrier.

V/STOL is not, and probably never will be, a substitute for the high performance conventional aircraft, but if it is a choice of aviation or no aviation, the former is better very time. The simple beauty of the V/STOL aircraft is that it does not condemn a fleet to building enormous flightdecks, for it can take off and be recovered on small decks or if necessary on no deck at all, and it can do it independently of wind direction. Many smaller fleets operating light carriers showed interest but even so it is doubtful if the British would ever have gone ahead with serious development had not the United States Marine Corps

Left:
Lynx successor — the Anglo Italian EH101, being developed by Westland and Agusta-Bell for service in the 1990s. Though this impression gives little idea of its size, its extra capability can be brought only at the expense of bulk and weight, putting it beyond the capacity of many current ships to stow it.
Westland Helicopters Ltd

Below:
First frigates to be designed with an organic helicopter, the British Type 81s were unique in housing it within an after deckhouse, a complex affair with elevator and folding roof. The resulting mast arrangement left much to be desired with the air and surface warning antenna blanketted by the adjacent lattice. *Mohawk* is seen at Gibraltar. *Mike Lennon*

(USMC) backed their convictions with cash for a substantial order.

Though the USMC was interested primarily in the capacity of the aircraft for ground support, its greatest potential for the smaller fleets is in countering the long-range air-launched anti-ship missile. Soviet doctrines embrace the co-ordinated use of these and both surface and sub-surface launched weapons, and the Americans make much of the need of their carrier-based aircraft to win the 'outer-area battle', destroying the aircraft that carry the weapons before they can get into launching range. Without its own aviation, however, a fleet could not even countenance an outer-area battle, relying instead on knocking the missiles down, once launched, with defence systems already saturated by the remaining threats.

For the moment the US Navy has kept V/STOL very much in what it sees as its place. Even so the cost of attaining and maintaining its goal of 15 flightdecks

suitably supported demand multi-billion dollar budgets. Each, once created, is so valuable a national asset that consideration must be given to how, and in what circumstances, it can be risked.

It is very likely that the long-running debate over the size of the 'ideal' American carrier would have favoured the so-called CVV of about 50,000 tons, thus breaking the awful progression to ever larger and more expensive decks, had not a new factor developed. Not for the first time, the Soviets adopted with enthusiasm a type of warship that apparently had had its day. As long as they had no carriers of their own, they vilified them. Eventually, their advancing techological capacity permitted them to build the 'Moskvas', heavily based on aforementioned French and Italian designs. They are primarily ASW-orientated but the leadship acted also as trials ship for the first operational Soviet V/STOL fighter, the Yak-36 ('Forger'). Like the British, the Russians discovered that such aircraft have much-improved endurance or payload if given a running take off. The full-width superstructure of the 'Moskvas' precluded this and the following 'Kievs' — true V/STOL carriers with neither catapults not arrester gear — have offset superstructure islands. They are first cousins to the British 'Invincibles', though of twice the displacement and of far greater offensive power.

The Soviet fleet is now, reportedly, at the next stage — the construction of an estimated 75,000-ton carrier with nuclear propulsion and full fixed-wing capability. With the entry into service of the first projected for the late 1980s the Americans will be forced to continue the construction of equivalents, for in this field capability is synonymous with survivability.

Smaller carriers, like smaller anything, smack also to many powerful American lobbies of being 'second best'. Elmo Zumwalt, one of the US Navy's most gifted seaman-planners, identified the need of a utility carrier, kept simple so as to be procurable in large numbers. This so-called Sea Control Ship (SCS) was commercially-designed — a single-screw workhorse and a logical successor to the escort carrier of the war years. Its functions were explored and proved in a modifed LPH. Had it been built, the SCS could have provided air support in low-hazard areas where a front-line carrier would be risked unnecessarily. It could have deployed ASW squadrons and been used for flightdeck training without needing to divert the large decks from their primary attack roles. In a protracted conventional war it would have been invaluable in support of the North Atlantic convoy routes. It would also have spread the US Navy's aviation around to the extent that the Soviets could

Left:
Over the unlikely setting of a seaside pier, a Royal Navy Sea Harrier carries a lethal load of Sea Eagle air-to-surface missiles. These, the first British weapons of their type, can be deployed also by shore-based Buccaneer and Tornado aircraft. Their active radar homing has a high degree of immunity to jamming.

Above:
The Super Frelon is a large helicopter used by the French Navy for ASW and minesweeping. It can also be used as a launch platform for the AM39 version of the Exocet, considerably extending the range and hitting power of the parent ship. It could, of course, equally well be deployed from ashore. *Aerospatiale*

Right:
An Exocet MM40 installation. *Aerospatiale*

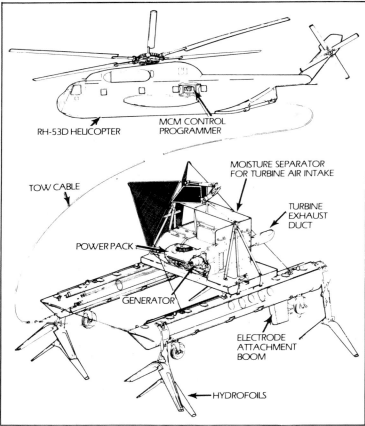

RH-53D HELICOPTER

MCM CONTROL PROGRAMMER

MOISTURE SEPARATOR FOR TURBINE AIR INTAKE

TOW CABLE

TURBINE EXHAUST DUCT

POWER PACK

GENERATOR

ELECTRODE ATTACHMENT BOOM

HYDROFOILS

Above:
A sizeable amphibious fleet can confer great flexibility. The USS *Nashville* is seen here flooded down and with stern gate partially lowered. Within the well are two 17.5m mine-sweeping boats (MSB) which, along with sleds towed by the RH-53D helicopters above, are used for inshore mine clearance.
L & L van Ginderen

Left:
Rapid coverage of an area sown with magnetic and/or acoustic mines is possible with the US Navy's Mk105 sweep gear. The sled, riding on its foils, is towed by the purpose-designed RH-53D helicopter. Aboard the sled is a generator whose function is to pulse the trailed sweep cable. Alternatively, an acoustic countermeasures device could be trailed. *EDO Corporation*

Right:
The Canadian Navy, with much accumulated ASW experience, pioneered the use of two large helicopters aboard a frigate, their extra capability being judged to be worth the effect on the ship's layout. Here, a Sea King is being hauled-down by the Bear Trap; once down, it will be towed to the hangar along the track visible in the deck.
Canadian Forces Photo

not contemplate a fully effective pre-emptive nuclear strike. But it was not built. Its sin was to be unable to operate the latest and largest of naval aircraft. It lacked the necessary 'pizzaz' to attract the funds away from the 'big deck' brigade, so the project withered and died. The Spanish Navy saw in it the answer to its own requirements and is currently building the first to the design; it is to be hoped that the *Principe de Asturias* will, on completion, prove the effectiveness of the concept, though this will not be easy with only one ship.

The need for seaborne aviation will not diminish, despite interminable Government White Papers. On the day, the fleet with air power on the spot will beat the fleet without it. Without a credible aviation element, a fleet would adopt a permanently defensive posture — unable to defeat either a direct assault by enemy air strike or indirect assault by his stand-off ASMs, unable to capitalise on the range of its own long-ranged weapons by virtue of difficulties in OTH targetting.

If the Royal Navy cannot have fixed-wing aircraft, it must have V/STOL carriers; if V/STOL technology is still at the 'string bag' stage then it must be developed. The resultant product would not only maintain the Navy as a credible force but have world-wide sales potential.

CHAPTER 6

Survivability, Versatility and Longevity

Warships are complex creations with a considerable degree of inter-activity between most of their desirable qualities, any of which may suffer in various degrees through over-concentration on the remainder. Taking, for example, those qualities that head this chapter if may readily be appreciated that a warship's capacity to survive may well be diminished by the requirement to make her as versatile as possible, ie general-purpose. It is not possible to forecast the particular threat that a ship may need to face and, statistically, she is likely to spend the greater part of her life fulfilling a police role in times of peace. The temptation to produce general-purpose ships and save money is therefore strong. As a result, more ships may be available to meet low-threat situations but more of them will be lost if forced to face a determined specialised threat.

Again, though this desirable across-the-board capability may save some money initially, this may not be true in the long term. During her expected life-span, a ship will need more than one major update if she is to retain her potency. By having more systems, however, there is a greater chance that obsolescence may occur, involving costly replacements or modernisations with more time out of service. If any of these changes are sufficiently radical they may result in it being considered cheaper to scrap or sell the ship and rebuild from scratch. Her disposal has not then been a function of her material state and she probably has many years of life potential left. In this case longevity has been adversely affected by the need for versatility. Increasingly, it is becoming the preserve of simpler ships to serve longest, these often wearing the flags of lower-order fleets which are not so exposed to the all-consuming blast of technological progress.

A continuing cause for surprise over recent years has been the way in which warships built during World War 2 have kept going. Most survivors are of American origin, their numbers reflecting not only the volume of the original production but also the quality of construction of their hulls and steam plant now 40 or more years of age. The many FRAM destroyers still serving with minor navies show how even thin-skinned hulls are not necessarily short-lived if their hearts are still sound. More impressive of course are the re-activated 'Iowa' class battleships

and the 'Salem' class super cruisers for which modernisation plans are also complete. Together with the many 'Midway' and 'Essex' class carriers, the last survivors of which are being phased out currently, they demonstrate the wisdom of sound maintenance on ships 'in ordinary'.

Mild steel of the war years was notoriously variable in quality and corrosion-related scrapping was frequent as early as the 1960s. There were in any case too many warships left from the massive war construction programmes and large-scale structural steel renewal was simply not economical. Even with the more rigid quality controls of peacetime, mild steel is compatible with the marine environment ony if separated from it by a thin and continuous protective film, usually paint. Maintaining this film is a continuous struggle that lasts the life of the ship; every rust streak is a token of a battle being lost. Despite its drawbacks, however, mild steel is still the only material that exhibits the ratio of cost to strength that allows use on a large scale. To avoid excessively large sections or weight, the designer may work-in high tensile steel of various grades in regions of known high stress, such as in the way of bilge and sheer strakes. Such special steels are of course more expensive and may not be so easily shaped, worked or

Above right:
Though the hull has years of life still in it, machinery, weapons and electronics are obsolete by first-line naval standards. Modernisation on peacetime budgets is uneconomic, so the ship is expended as a target: HMS *Devonshire* after a direct hit from a Sea Eagle SSM. The explosion from within has blown out some 15m of shell plating and almost certainly disabled machinery spaces. Fire would have resulted in an operational ship which, while still afloat, would have had to be scuttled. *British Aerospace Dynamics*

Right:
First line fleets, though working their ships hard, keep them in very good order so that when they become obsolete they still have many years of service left in them. For instance 'Friesland' class destoyers, replaced in the Netherlands navy by 'Standaard' frigates, have found a ready market in Peru. Here, the *Overijssel* at den Helder puts up her new pendants as the *Bolognesi*. *L & L van Ginderen*

welded. Among other qualities they must show compatibility with the mild steels that they complement and must not fail by brittle fracture when cyclicly stressed by ship movement under conditions of extreme cold. That such problems may not manifest themselves immediately was demonstrated some years ago when West Germany's first postwar submarines, whose hulls were constructed of amagnetic steel to reduce the signature seen by MAD and magnetic mines, needed to be virtually reconstructed after some years of service due to metallurgical failure.

Never can too much attention be paid to the preparation of a steel surface prior to its painting for no amount of subsequent topcoats will offset the deficiencies. An area of plate, working in a seaway, may lift its paintwork through the adhesion breaking down with the differential elasticity of skin and substrate. Paint may be chipped, scored and abraded by a hundred agencies — the damage spreading rapidly if not treated quickly. Along the waterline paint has to contend with continual impact with the sea, particularly forward, and the scour of particles suspended in the water along the boundary layer in general. Cavitation occurs not only at obvious points but potentially at any discontinuity, even including

plate laps and proud weld seams, where again the paint can be removed by what equates to a gentle but continuous shot-blasting.

Why then not use a non-rusting aluminium alloy? The same arguments are often used for the family car and can generally be rejected on the same grounds; although aluminium is little more than one-third the density of steel it usually requires the same weight overall to achieve the same strength and rigidity and is very much more expensive and more difficult to work. Aluminium hulls, like those of wood, are limited by the material's properties to a maximum size, and lengths in excess of 60m are rare.

Suitably alloyed with materials such as magnesium or lithium, aluminium can be considerably enhanced in its properties. It is quite commonly used in the superstructures of large vessels with steel hulls, particular attention needing to be paid to the junction between the two dissimilar metals where in the presence of salt water corrosion and failure will easily occur. Lighter superstructures are a real bonus when it is recalled how hull-mounted weight in the form of heavy machinery and armouring has disappeared from modern hulls in the process of development while at the same time superstructures have become more voluminous. A serious drawback of structural aluminium alloys is their capacity to burn fiercely once exposed to the intense heat of electrical arcing, an explosion or the fireball created by the unspent fuel and oxydiser within an SSM that scores a direct hit. Furthermore, where steel tends to tear on being hit, aluminium can shatter and cause splinter damage while itself being easily pierced by splinters from another source. Some high speed craft such as FACs are of aluminium alloy or wood clad on alloy frames but the majority are of thin welded steel. Only for

Above:
It is always better to keep the SSM out than try and tackle the results. Here a target ship displays the result of an Exocet hit, possibly from the 'Combattante III' FAC in the background. The damage is typical of an SSM hit on a thin-skinned modern warship, taking out a complete section above the waterline. Should the victim not be destroyed by fire or structural failure, she would almost certainly have to scuttled under combat conditions. *Aerospatiale*

Left:
Fire in warships is often accompanied by dense and noxious smoke and survival may well depend on rapid identification of the seat of the problem. The rugged, man-portable EEV Thermal Imaging Camera can accompany a fire-fighting team, 'seeing' infra-red energy which is of a wavelength short enough to penetrate the densest smoke. *EEV*

highly weight-critical vessels such as hydrofoils or surface-effect craft is aluminium alloy virtually mandatory. No other metals would seem at the moment to become candidates to replace steel and aluminium in general use.

Though the non-magnetic properties of aluminium alloys would be valuable for vessels such as mine warfare ships, few have ever been built of it, it having been more common to use wood planks on alloy frames. Wooden frames need to be grown or laminated and are consequently expensive, but wood cladding can be very durable if properly maintained and is resilient to the shock of nearby explosions.

Top:
**Spot the join. HMS *Wilton* was the world's first major
warship constructed from glass-reinforced plastic (GRP).
Comparing her with the identical view of the wooden-built
Kirkliston on Page 80 it is difficult to see any difference.
Fitted-out with standard CMS components she paved the way
for the 'Hunt' class MCMVs.** *Mike Lennon*

Above:
**Localised heating during the welding process causes plate
distortion known as 'starved dog' — very obvious on large
expanses of hull such as that of the 5,440-ton destroyer *Fife*.
Interestingly, a replacement plate immediately below the
4.5in gun barrels shows as a smooth rectangle.** *Mike Lennon*

Unfortunately the number of small shipyards capable
of working competently in wood is decreasing rapidly.
Aluminium would therefore have been set to become
more widely used in this area but for the fast
development of techniques in glass-reinforced plastic
(GRP) construction. Paradoxically, the loss of
expertise in wood craftsmanship has largely paralleled
the rise in popularity of GRP, mainly because the
smaller woodworking yards base their activities on
the pleasure boat market, where GRP has made its
greatest impact.

GRP was for too long confined to smaller hulls
because its strength was extremely variable, largely
because mixing and laying-up were usually inconsis-
tent. The British appreciated its potential if it could
only be worked under controlled conditions. A
coastal minesweeper (CMS) was selected as a
prototype to evaluate the material, even this modest
size of hull representing a considerable extra-
polation of existing techniques and known data. A
full-size section of an existing design was therefore
built to establish the likely problems — what was the
philosophy, for instance, of designing a frame integral
with the skin? How critical was environmental control
on mixes? How could the application process be
enlarged to make construction on this scale feasible?
Would there be health problems when dealing with
irritating fumes and substances on a large scale? As

the available data for such a new material was far from comprehensive, design erred on the generous side and the finished structure was then heavily stressed and fatigue-cycled in a purpose-built frame. This was the stage at which various design changes and practices could also be evaluated and compared. Sufficient data won, a full-sized GRP replica of a 'Ton' class hunter was ordered from Vosper Thornycroft. It took considerable time to design and construct the required covered facility and then to develop techniques for what was a brand new concept in warship construction, but the ship that resulted, HMS *Wilton*, was highly satisfactory and enabled the Ministry of Defence to commit itself rapidly to the new 'Brecon' class MCMVs so urgently needed to replace ships already 30 and more years of age. It was something of an act of faith to commit so much to the facility but the decision was fully vindicated and a second one was set up at Yarrow, Glasgow to assist in series production. Following the lead and no doubt benefiting from others' hard won experience, France, Belgium and the Netherlands have set up largely similar facilities to produce the so-called Tripartite MCMV, with Italy going it alone. Interestingly, the United States and Germany (the former with their

mine countermeasures forces run down to a state of virtual non-existence) were carried along with this belated quickening of interest but are apparently playing cautiously by sticking to traditional wood on alloy. West Germany has yards well versed in and still geared to such construction but the US decision may well be politically based.

Shipbuilding methods have changed as drastically for warships as they have for merchantmen. Traditionally a keel was laid from which gradually arose an elegant tapestry of floors and longitudinals, frames, stringers and beams. On to this complex framework was then rivetted the decks, bulkheads and skin. It made for strong and pretty construction but was geared to an age when labour was cheap and time seldom of great consequence. The massive and

Below:
Big as a house, several hundred tons of bow section of the American carrier *Theodore Roosevelt* is inched into position. The module is in an advanced state of internal fitting-out before incorporation as are the remainder that comprise the 332m hull. *Newport News Shipbuilding*

urgent programmes of World War 2 changed all that. Welding had been cautiously introduced during the 1930s mainly as a means of saving weight in designs built to tight Treaty limits. Rivetted construction, by its very nature, demanded much extra metal through plates being either lapped or joined by straps. Welding united the plates edge-to-edge, cutting out the weight of the overlaps and the rivets themselves. The inbuilt weakness of rivets to shear off or weep was also cured, though their ability to 'give' slightly in a seaway was held by many to be an advantage lost with the stiff and unyielding welded hulls. Certainly, when welding first began to be used on a large scale, there were many cases of major failures, with numerous ships (mainly mercantile) breaking in two, some even under the bending stresses generated by discharging cargo. Another time-consuming and extremely noisy operation rendered unnecessary by welding was caulking. With smooth transitions from plate to plate, and with raised weld seams suitably dressed, a hull also offered less skin resistance.

One loss, however, was the near-perfect curvature of the plating, the harmony of which on a rivetted hull produced an effect that was a delight to the eye. In its place, the built-in stresses left by the localised heat of the welder's electrode caused plates to indent between frames, leaving an effect known widely as 'starved dog'. These slight departures from fairness are not usually of much import but do add to the skin friction below the waterline and add nothing to the ship's appearance above it.

Welding was the essential ingredient of the new concept of modular construction. In place of the extended building process on the ship, with each task being performed in serial in all weathers, ships were to be composed of numerous sub-assemblies, or modules, carefully toleranced so as to be capable of mating into a whole. Only the final assembly needed to be carried out on a slip, or eventually in a covered building dock. The modules themselves could be constructed in equable conditions under cover, guaranteeing good workmanship untroubled by

CHAFF

Missile warning I.R. Decoy fired creating diversion close to ship Chaff decoy ejected.

I.R.

I.R. decoy maintained and extended by second-phase ejection of parachute-borne grenades at increasing ranges.

Chaff cloud and I.R. decoys attract missile from ship taking evasive action.

Left:
Protean is one of several systems designed to be activated automatically by the detection of an incoming SSM. While it is effective against active and semi-active sea skimmers, those with television homing systems or capable of terminal diving would pose further problems. *MEL*

Right:
Contrasting vividly with the noise and ordered chaos of the building slip in the traditional shipyard is the covered facility of today, which permits work to continue irrespective of weather conditions. Launches have become 'float-outs' with the ship in an advanced state of completion. The Dutch *Jacob van Heemskerck* is here ready to make way for the next in the programme, the *Witte de With*.
Royal Schelde

extremes of weather, and delivered to the main assembly hall in an advanced state of fitting out, this being achieved in conditions of maximum accessibility. Modules did not even have to be constructed on site, for instance the German U-boat programme received sections of pressure hulls from sub-contractors around the country, transported to the shipyard by inland waterway.

Progress since the war has been rapid, due largely to the commercial development of production-line construction techniques for such as VLCCs during their hey-day. Individual modules weighing several hundred tons each are common, moved around on special low-loaders. Smaller modules can be 'walked' around on hydraulics or hovered on air cushions. Goliath cranes straddle both building berth and assembly/delivery areas, lifting apartment-block-sized fabrications on a delicate web of wire and locating them deliberately and with pin-point accuracy at their desired billets. Warships up to destroyer size are commonly assembled in covered building halls of

much the same layout, being launched or floated-out in an advanced state of completion. Such is the flexibility of modern construction that, if the covered part of the slip is too short for a particular type of ship, her stern can first be set up and lengthened by successive sections working forward, at each stage jacking the part ship further down the slip to make room, a process known as extrusion. For all but the largest ships, expensive dry docks and permanent slips can be superseded by such as the Synchrolift, a platform which can be moved vertically, supported and guided by numerous pillars. Once the platform is lowered a ship can be manoeuvred over it and then lifted bodily out of the water. Supported on bogies, it can then be transferred by track and even translated sideways to a desired site for work to be undertaken, freeing the capital-intensive lift for further operation.

Due to the much lighter scale of construction of the modern warship, much heavy engineering involved in the bending and forming of thick plates and sections has been dispensed with. Rolling sections of

submarine hulls and their subsequent welding remains a specialist area due to the weight and types of steel used, and the particularly high standards of quality control that are applied.

Both design methods and building plant have been revolutionised. Ship designers no longer labour at drawing boards, but before a visual display unit, 'drawing' with cursor and menu tablet or 'number crunching' with the keyboard. The ubiquitous computer performs the actions that he puts upon it, displaying the result and considering the alternatives as necesary. Once the desired solution has been achieved, the data will be digitised to produce control tapes which will guide the machines that will cut the metal. Cutter heads will move automatically, instruments of an unseen hand, producing sets of handed plates, nested neatly to minimise waste. Welding, for the greater part, is also carried out under preset and controllable conditions by machine. Shipbuilding will never be a clean job, not particularly quiet, but the all-pervading smoke and steam, and the raucous din of the caulkers' and riveters' hammers are now largely a thing of the past.

A modern ship would be considered ludicrously flimsy by a seaman of even a half-century past but then the war at sea has itself changed. Ships of the size required can no more be protected to keep out the massive energy content of an SSM than the smaller ships of a generation before could prevent penetration by a 16in shell. Weapons themselves have to be kept out, countered by soft or hard kill techniques as appropriate; any attempt at real armouring would rapidly escalate the ship's size with unmentionable effects on the cost. One hit is therefore very likely to prove fatal. Even if the missile warhead fails to detonate, as in the recent case of HMS *Sheffield*, a strike can cause a devastating fire. Vital points of centralised control are very likely to be destroyed or severely damaged, effectively putting

Below:
Alongside the fitting-out berth at Vlissengen, an air defence version of the Standaard, *Jacob van Heemskerck*, contrasts with the AS unit *Pieter Florisz*. Note the high freeboard taken right aft, no hangar, larger casings on the bridge front for the Sea Sparrow reload system and the target designator antenna on the foremast, just visible against the crane structure behind. *Royal Schelde*

the ship out of the battle even without sinking her. Decentralisation of a ship's essential functions will aid survivability but no point can be considered safe. The Falklands Conflict again showed how little resistance the modern, thin-skinned ship has to cannon-fire and splinter damage, and it is becoming the practice to 'harden' vital components such as waveguides and cable runs. While aluminium and composite armouring is available for this, the popular current material is an aramid fibre known by the proprietary name of Kevlar which can be supplied as rigid laminates or woven into a range of flexible blankets, with a weight penalty only half that of equivalent steel protection. Even so, one is talking about mechanical protection only from fragments or small calibre automatic fire.

Further 'hardening' needs to be provided against the somewhat ill-defined effects of the electro-magnetic pulse, or EMP, that follows a nuclear explosion. The enormous amount of electrical energy released into the atmosphere is capable of generating very high instantaneous local potentials in unprotected circuits, capable of burning-out components and leaving the ship without vital systems. Even without such damage, however, few communications systems or sensors are likely to be operable for a considerable period in the immediate area of a burst.

The effects of explosion-induced shock are still difficult to quantify and design-out so it remains the practice to submit the first of a new class of vessel to quite severe shock testing by detonating charges in close proximity and studying the results, the lessons of which can then be incorporated into the remainder of the class.

Warships can be incapacitated through fire or action damage but, to be sunk, they still have to be flooded. As far as is possible a hull will be compartmentalised to contain flooding by watertight bulkheads, paying particular attention to routes by which the hull may progressively flood as it trims and settles. Ships may be designed to a standard which would permit, say, any two adjacent compartments to be flooded without sinking or capsizing, but survival depends largely on weather conditions and tactical circumstances, or whether more water has had to be admitted to the hull, either in fire-fighting or to counterflood by way of correcting a dangerous list or trim. A useful device in this connection is an adaptation of the micro-computerised Loadmaster, long available to mercantile chief officers. Commer-ically it is programmed to calculate bending moment and trim resulting from any theoretical order in loading and discharging cargo spaces. With suitable adaptation, it could be tailored to a particular warship, giving invaluable advice to the damage control officer of the results and/or consequence of various decisions that could be implemented.

Ships may also be capable of operating for specified periods within areas of contamination caused by nuclear, bacteriological or chemical weapons. To do this, they must incorporate citadel areas, enclosing personnel and vulnerable services in an atmosphere that is either cleaned and filtered or slightly over-pressured for the duration, over which the external surfaces of the vessel are automatically washed down from permanent mains. The ability of modern warships to run with unattended and remotely monitored and controlled machinery spaces is an important factor in the creation of such citadels.

Damage control is all too often looked upon as some sort of 'Cinderella' occupation. It is not. Familiarity with the ship and a determination to fight for both her and their survival is instilled into every crewmember. Regular blindfold escape drills, wearing personnel breathing apparatus when available, engenders crew confidence in finding 'the way out' in an emergency but equally regular 'evolutions' to counter the full spectrum of possible situations are also important. The sea outside is a hostile environment; fighting to save the ship is both morale-boosting and, ultimately, life-saving.

It is probably in a real emergency that the trends towards cutting crew numbers will prove disadvantageous. Though in some situations, such as a deep-seated fire, it may be necessary to evacuate all non-essential manpower, this pre-supposes help at hand. The crisis could equally well result from a mine or torpedo, or from a natural hazard such as heavy weather or stranding. On countless occasions a goodly-sized crew has still worked itself to exhaustion for days, pumping and even baling, shoring bulkheads, plugging holes and restoring services before eventually winning through. Today's small and technically orientated crews are often deficient in the basic seamanship on which the 'old' navy ran. Fitness is sometimes not of the highest order — the comfort and excellent messing deemed necessary to keep the 'right' sort of man at sea, separated from normal life, also takes its toll on physical toughness.

CHAPTER 7

The Impact of Cost

Toward the end of the 18th Century, about the time when Bligh was being parted from the *Bounty* and the Royal Navy was gearing itself up for involvement in the French Revolutionary War, a three-decked, 100-gun First Rate could be built and fitted-out for sea for a sum that would leave change out of £70,000. Barely 70 years later, the Navy entered the ironclad era with the single-decked *Warrior*, which cost five times as much and nearly bankrupted the builders. The Edwardian naval budget creaked under the weight of the £1.75 million bill for the *Dreadnought* but, today, even a warship as unremarkable as a Type 22 (of about the same overall length as the *Warrior*) costs upward of £130 million. If that level of expenditure catches the breath, the equivalent figures from the USA are acquiring just too many zeroes to grasp at all. At 1982 levels, a 'Nimitz' class CVN costs about $2 billion and a Trident-armed SSBN about half as much. Even with an annual naval appro-priation in excess of $10 billion, only a few such vessels can be contemplated in addition to everything else.

Constrained by tighter spending limits, planners need to address two main questions: what is the likely role of the fleet in 5, 10 or 20 years time? How many and of what kind of ship will be needed to discharge that role? With respect to the first, it should be remembered that a first of class may be a decade or more in gestation, so sudden changes of course are not easy and inflation makes hay of budget estimates.

Definition of the future role of a fleet is not easy and parsimonious peacetime Treasuries are always both ready and able to make a nonsense of the exercise. This was all too recently demonstrated by an emaciated Royal Navy's difficulty in controlling even a minor South Atlantic fleet. *The Way Ahead* had pointed to total involvement with NATO, inferiority of surface warships compared with nuclear sub-

Left:
Foreign deployments of older American SSBNs are made possible by specialised tenders that can service both engineering and weaponry. Here the *Edison* (SSBN-610) offloads a missile via the gantry crane of the tender *Hunley* (AS-31) at Holy Loch in Scotland. While the larger ship is listing under the load, the rigid mooring arrangement prevents mutual shift between the hulls during this delicate operation.

Right:
Proof of the folly of designing to unrealistic low budgets, HMS *Manchester* is a Type 42 destroyer of a design necessarily 'stretched' to achieve its original object. Post-Falklands War modifications include trading seaboats for extra light guns and decoy projectors, less black paint topside and a greatly improved surveillance radar. *Mike Lennon*

marines and the redundancy of a fleet amphibious element. This narrow, clinical, accountant's view was brutally exposed as ignoring the inherent flexibility of the surface warship, to which the fleet submarine is complementary and not a substitute. It ignored the fact that, because of their cost, fewer of such submarines could be built and, no matter how good at their particular job, cannot be in more than one place at a time. It ignored any out-of-area commitment, an eventuality best met by sea. It ignored the fact that the British Merchant Marine had been virtually halved in seven years of slump, and trading in competition with government-subsidised and protected foreign-flag ships. Finally, it ignored the lessons of history, still valid in spite of increasingly computerised opinion. The upshot could have been disastrous.

Others, too, are not beyond criticism of the manner in which budgets are spent. Much American ink has been spilt on the theory of a two-ocean navy with the correct 'Hi-Lo' mix; having elaborated on this, however, the lion's share of funding goes to the powerful lobbies of the 'big three' — carriers, aviation and nuclear submarines. Large nuclear carriers are superb weapon platforms, but their justification automatically justifies also top quality aviation, escorts and support ships. The navy's target of 15 fast carrier groups is laudable but not at the expense of the less glamorous but equally needed ocean ASW escorts to cover the vital NATO resupply convoy route or the mine countermeasures forces to meet the inevitable Soviet onslaught on American coastal routes and ports. Scant regard seems to have been paid to the fact that the Soviets are hardly likely to 'play fair' and, from Day One, will opt for low-yield nuclear weapons on each carrier group at sea, obliterating each with little attendant risk of escalating to a general nuclear conflict on land. A

larger number of smaller flight decks would give the fleet a better chance of surviving an all-out pre-emptive strike in a shape to continue the fight. Their inevitable lower capability would stimulate a rapid improvement in the aviation to complement them.

Attack submarines also are getting ever larger and more expensive for, apparently, only marginal improvements in offensive power. Smaller alternatives and the complementary, but highly capable, diesel-electric conventional vessels are barely considered.

It will be obvious from the foregoing that this first and fundamental stage of fleet role identification should be undertaken imaginatively and thoroughly; all shades of opinion should be heard and deaf ears turned to lobbying by vested interests. The results should be binding, but reviewed regularly.

With the mix of ships identified, the characteristics of each need to be defined. Possibly a required type does not even exist and may need to be developed. An example is the current (1984) need by the British for a vessel to deploy a flight of four or five AS helicopters in the South Atlantic. Unlimited budgets may well have encouraged a prototype SWATH ship (see also Chapter 11) — an exotic solution that would have met the requirement and, maybe, started a whole new line of naval development. Instead, the Ministry of Defence decided to apply the experience of the *Arapaho* project in chartering a medium-sized container ship, fitting her with a temporary flightdeck and ISO container-sized modular back-up facilities. Resulting directly from limited available funds, the solution will appear ad hoc but gives further valuable experience in the development of an eventual mercantile-style fleet for use in lower-risk areas, a possibility also discussed in Chapter 11.

Initially, cheap warships may balance an annual

Above:
Cost, machinery, helicopters and a near-standard armament conspire together to make ASW frigate designs remarkably similar. Noticeable on this official model of the projected Canadian frigate *Halifax* is the siting of the helicopter facilities right aft — unlike earlier practice — and the unusual (and, presumably, low visibility) mast.
Canadian Forces Photo

Left:
With fewer warships available, high quality merchantment will need to be capable of a measure of self help and, in many cases, available for conversion to auxiliary warships. The British Aerospace SCADS (A) system turns a container ship into a helicopter carrier with point defence. Other schemes provide for fully containerised defence systems for merchantmen, V/STOL capacity and conversion to amphibious assault support. *British Aerospace*

budget but the price may well be more in the long term, in awkwardness of repair, lower availability and inferior capability. With this in mind, the Life Cycle cost is far more realistic a figure than the so-called Unit Price Cost, but is not easily calculated realistically. Both the British Types 22 and 42 can be quoted as examples of ships built to an over-constricting budget. Each design has had to be stretched in order to accommodate a worthwhile armament. Successive classes of warship also tend to be more expensive even in real terms. Reasons for this include improvements in standards, not only in construction but also in the crew's conditions. Moreover, ships become more capable and complex, major motivating factors in the noticeably cyclic nature of warship development.

Standards need to be high for various reasons. To attract the right people, conditions afloat have to be good. At the same time, however, crewmen are expensive in terms of both pay and impact on the ship herself, needing living space, services and catering. All these demand space, making the ship larger without enhancing her fighting qualities. The role of each person afloat needs to be examined, for in such areas as combining duties in flexible rostering, adding appropriate automation and designing for minimum maintenance requirements at sea, numbers may be reduced. Even so, there has to be a minimum for effective damage control and to maintain extensive periods at full alert when necessary.

High standards in seaworthiness are a good investment. For a relatively small initial outlay in a longer hull and stabilisers, the ship will have a less violent motion, resulting in a less fatigued and therefore more efficient crew. The ship will suffer less damage from the sea and will continue as an effective

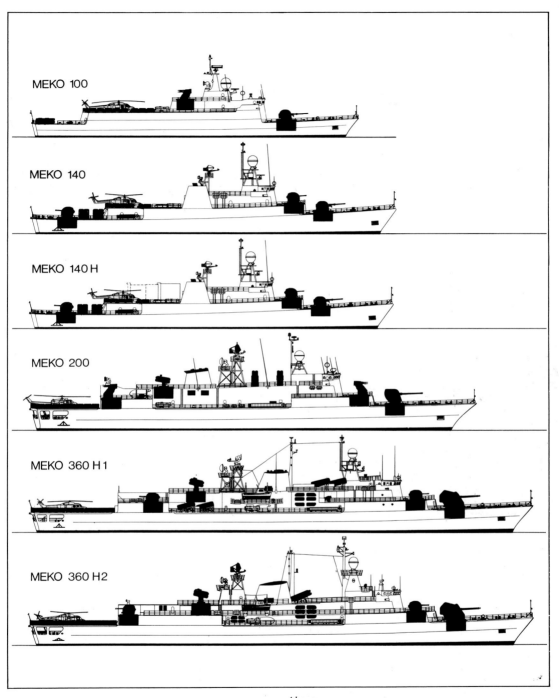

MEKO 100

MEKO 140

MEKO 140 H

MEKO 200

MEKO 360 H 1

MEKO 360 H 2

Above:
**Blohm and Voss' complete current MEKO range with their
modular components accented. Economics demand that this
approach to warship construction makes sense and
manufacturers may increasingly be obliged to design with an
eye to modularisation of their products.** *Blohm & Voss AG*

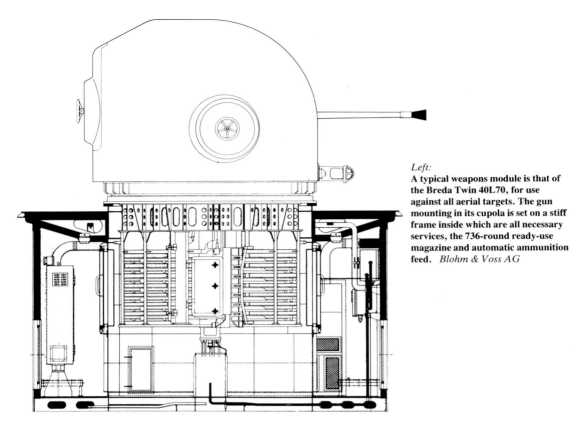

Left:
A typical weapons module is that of the Breda Twin 40L70, for use against all aerial targets. The gun mounting in its cupola is set on a stiff frame inside which are all necessary services, the 736-round ready-use magazine and automatic ammunition feed. *Blohm & Voss AG*

fighting unit into far more extreme conditions. Increased availability results in the need for fewer ships to do the same amount of work or a greater capability from the same number of hulls. Longer ships are more economically propelled, offer a better layout topsides, lower superstructures, internal space for subsequent updating and machinery layout that will survive action damage.

Reduction in self-generated noise is never bought cheaply but is vital to improve the performance of one's own sensors while at the same time, rendering one less liable to detection by an enemy. Hull and propeller design need to be optimised, machinery carefully selected and mounted.

Cost escalation can result from succeeding classes becoming progressively more eleborate, a tendency exhibited by many navies. A good example is afforded by the FAC. When the Soviets suddenly introduced the Styx SSM in the late 1950s and sent it to sea in the *Komars*, they stole a march on the West, producing over 100 cheap boats of only 80 tons apiece yet capable of disabling a cruiser out to horizon range. Viewed as expendable, they were distributed liberally among friendly powers and produced a major headache on vital Western sea routes for minimum outlay. Obviously such small craft had limitations, but the purpose-built 'Osa's' that

followed leapt from a 27m to a 30m hull, doubled installed power for a lower speed and required over 30 crew in place of 11. Carrying four SSMs, they also had better endurance and seaworthiness. But in turn they became a less expendable asset, demanding a more powerful defensive armament.

Western-designed FACs stemmed directly from this stimulus, but were built around four of the only proven available SSM — the bulky MM38 Exocet. A combination of these, and a questionable insistence on a 76mm gun required a hull of at least 47m overall yet the vessel was still highly vulnerable to aircraft attack. An example is the West German Type 148, whose seakeeping and C3 facilities were then improved to produce the Type 143, an expensive 57m craft with a complement of 40. Still as open to attention from the air, reliance was placed on the thin reed of shore-based aircraft support and only with the latest group, the 143As, has a cheap point defence SAM system been introduced.

With the American Harpoon and the MM40 version of Exocet came SSMs compact enough to make possible the fitting of six or eight to an FAC. While doubling firepower, their extra range conferred an over-the-horizon (OTH) capability — but only if mid-course correction was available. The Israelis have been first to respond by building craft with a

small helicopter, but stowage and a necessarily moderate ship motion for operation have escalated length to 62m. This type of craft, together with the very different Soviet 'Nanuchka', is moving the FAC into the corvette bracket — within the means of far fewer fleets. History has afforded other such examples, notably the destroyer and the aircraft carrier. Growth in complexity, capability and cost lead eventually to the extinction of the type or transition to a new beginning.

For a frigate-sized ship, about one third of the total initial cost will be accounted for by armament and related systems. Main and auxiliary machinery together with electrics demand an only slightly smaller proportion. Only some 15% is dedicated to the ship to house them, a fact that has two significant corollaries: firstly, ships are far less expensive than

their contents, so larger hulls, with all their advantages, are not luxuries beyond price, secondly, scope for construction economies is limited. Thin plating saves weight but requires many stiffeners. Simple rather than complex curvature of hull plating is less acceptable aesthetically but can produce savings without detracting significantly from the efficiency of a well-designed hull.

Technology is advancing at an ever higher rate and, for a warship to remain viable, it will probably need several updates in the course of a 25-year life span. Early 'Leanders' cost the Royal Navy about £4.7 million in the mid 1960s. A decade later, the last of the class were commanding a price of near £7 million. Cost of mid-life modernisation has since rocketed to about £70 million — a figure so horrifying as to rule out updating the final few units or, indeed, any at all

Above:
**An air-to-surface AM 39 version of the Exocet slung beneath a
Mirage fighter-bomber, which is fitted also with auxiliary
tanks and air-to-air missiles. The air-launched Exocet was a
major threat to British naval forces during the Falklands war
of 1982 — not because suitable countermeasures did not exist,
but because economies had determined their non-
availability.** *Aerospatiale*

of the Type 42s. With these costing some £120 million
in 1983, the prospect of no mid-life refit is one of
distinctly wasted assets and a radical change of view is
required to alter this unsatisfactory trend.

The basis of one such change has existed for some
time in modular construction techniques. Advantages
have been demonstrated by the British, with the
so-called Cellularity System, and by the Americans,
initially with SEAMOD, and later the Sea Systems
Engineering Standards or SSES. None has yet been
translated into actual metal and it has been left to a
private shipbuilder, Blohm and Voss of Hamburg, to
prove the concept. Their MEKO (Mehrzweck-
kombination or Multi-function) family of warships
consists of a standard range of hulls with framed
apertures into which a variety of weapons and sensors
can be fitted. Each of these assemblies is complete in
itself and needs only to be hooked into the ship's
supplies and set up. For a small penalty in extra steel
the ship can be effectively kitted-out for a particular
mission from a store of fully-maintained gear,

spending only a minimum of time alongside a
dockyard wall. Hulls, weapons and sensors can be
procured separately in numbers and at times suited to
command the greatest economies. Shorter refit times
mean greater availability and, possibly, fewer
necessary hulls as a result. There is obviously a
realistic limit to interchangeability but the idea is
worthy of wider application.

That capability can be improved fairly cheaply was
proved in the American 'Spruance' class. Widely
criticised as underarmed by the uninformed, they
mount the weapons fit of a 4,000-tonner on twice the
displacement, the big hull being far more weatherly
and able to conduct ASW in far more extreme
conditions. Space also abounds for future updating.
The 'Spruance' programme, like that of recent US
frigate classes, has been the subject of block
procurement — the design, construction, commis-
sioning and initial maintenance being made the
province of one, or very few, builders. This procedure
offers advantages in supply, support, training and
production costs though such extended programmes
in inflation-ridden times results inevitably in much
legal wrangling over later escalation clauses. Even
with a purpose-built ship facility, labour mobility
between various units is a problem and design effort
tends to peak inconveniently. For such long
production runs the navy, on one hand, prefers the
incorporation of well-tried systems for reliability
while still looking for the latest technology to prevent
the onset of obsolescence any earlier than is
avoidable. Truly, the designers lot is not an easy one.

CHAPTER 8

Stealth, Seakindliness and Manoeuvrability

In the uncompromising world of hunters and hunted, stealth may be the only factor that prevents the one becoming the other. A natural predator uses its senses to locate and stalk its prey; in the terminology of the trade, the prey possesses 'signatures' which may be detected by the predator's sensors, ie it may be seen, heard, smelled, tasted or touched. Obviously, it can reduce its visual signature by standing end-on as opposed to broadside-on but, perhaps less obviously, a ship may equally well reduce her radar cross-section or even heat signature by doing the same thing and, perhaps, puzzling an incoming missile. Much can also be done at the design stage to reduce the radar reflective potential of a ship. By approaching from down-wind, a hunter reduces the effect of scent and sound, the self-evident result of thousands of years of practice. In short, the successful hunter takes care not to advertise his presence in any way. Ships are no different.

Not only can a ship be seen or heard, however, she also produces heat, magnetic fields and pressure patterns, any of which can be detected by the right sensor and used to turn her into yet another target. It is part of the exhaustive process of warship design to reduce these unquantifiables to a minimum.

Noise is a many-sided failing. In human terms, the crew's efficiency is reduced by its causing annoyance, distraction and fatigue through disturbance of leisure time and sleep. Noise is also radiated out into the surrounding water and whereas its higher-frequency content may be rapidly attenuated, lower frequencies may carry for considerable distances, enabling a silent and listening enemy to detect the presence of the ship and conferring upon him the choice of whether to attack or escape. In the former case, the same noise that betrayed the ship may well be the means of homing-in a weapon.

Surface ships make a certain amount of unavoidable noise as they impact the sea, their structure creaking and groaning under the imposed stresses. Not surprisingly, a hull-mounted sonar may well have its performance thus degraded, having difficulty in separating tiny incoming signals from the ambient sea, a situation akin to two people 50yd apart in a football crowd endeavouring to hold a conversation. A submarine, running quietly and deep, is not so affected and is a very effective sonar platform.

Other noise can be reduced by good design. Machinery is a prime source, for where gas or steam turbines are well balanced and smooth-running, reciprocating engines such as diesels can be troublesome. Whether prime movers or auxiliaries, they are best raft-mounted and isolated from the hull by resilient supports.

Propellers are perhaps the most distinctive sources of noise. The near-symmetrical after sections of a submerged submarine enable its large-diameter propeller to turn in something approaching an ideal wake of near even cross-section. Again, however, the surface ship compares unfavourably. She probably has two propellers, of necessity of smaller diameter and more heavily loaded. They turn in an asymmetric flow on one side of the ship, their clearance to the underside of the ship's plating may be small and they are close enough to the surface for a significant pressure gradient to exist vertically across the disc from static water head. Turning in so confused an environment, propellers are likely to emit a rhythmic beat with a frequency compounded of shaft speed and the number of blades. Good design, to optimise flow through the propeller disc, is essential at an early stage. Failure can result in a complex noise signature of propellers and machinery that can not only identify the class but even individual ships within it.

Poor propeller, as opposed to hull, design can end in a screw 'singing' or cavitating. 'Singing' is a high frequency vibration, the only desirable cure for which is sometimes manufacture from a special non-resonant alloy. Cavitation forms particularly on propellers but it can also be associated with fixed appendages or discontinuities in the hull. It can occur anywhere that the pressure distribution creates a region where the absolute pressure drops below the vapour pressure of the surrounding water. In a process often compared with 'cold water boiling', small vapour pockets are formed only to immediately collapse. A characteristic noise is emitted, surfaces are eroded and in the case of propellers a drop in efficiency results. Even as far back as World War 2, German acoustic torpedoes were able to distinguish between merchantmen and their escorts.

The current state-of-the-art in micro-electronics has produced weapons of the calibre of the American CAPTOR mines. Essentially an encapsulated homing

Above:
High freeboard, low profile. The British Type 12 frigate
Scarborough **belonged to the first generation of post-war fast AS ships which, incorporating wartime lessons, sought to combine speed and seaworthiness with reduced visibility and vulnerability to nuclear blast effect. Note that the nuclear submarine had not yet necessitated the helicopter.**
Mike Lennon

torpedo, it can be moored in deep water or bottom laid. Its passive sensors listen to, and analyse, the signatures of passing ships. The analysis is compared with those of desired targets stored in an on-board data bank. When a signature tallies, the torpedo is released. This level of discrimination is likely to increase and it behoves the naval designer well to minimise noise from any source.

Magnetism is something with which every ferrous ship has to live. Unfortunately, it can be exploited to trigger a magnetic mine, explode a torpedo warhead as it passes beneath the keel of a surface ship or betray the presence of a submerged submarine to an aircraft flying overhead. The process of building a ship causes her to become a magnet and where, during World War 2, it was sufficient either to 'wipe' the hull or to give permanent immunity through a degaussing girdle around the hull, modern weaponry demands more sophisticated techniques. The magnetic field of a warship is complex and three-dimensional, varying constantly with different combinations of machinery in use at any one time. It can be checked on a purpose-built range and an active electrical generator system installed which will provide the necessary current flow through various permanently installed coils in the hull to neutralise the ship's field.

If a ship is expected to operate at length in waters likely to be mined, further measures can be taken. Mine countermeasures vessels (MCMV) can be built of wood or glass-reinforced plastic (GRP) even having engines of non-ferrous alloys. Steels for submarine hulls can be amagnetic, though, in the case of at least one West German type, this carried a penalty of metallurgical problems.

In spite of all care being taken, however, a metal ship rolling rapidly in a seaway can still become a crude dynamo — a coil cutting the flux of the earth's magnetic field — with small currents being set up in the hull. The small potential differences involved can be detected, amplified and made to trigger a mine.

Heat radiates energy in the infra-red region of the spectrum. A ship is invariably warmer than her surroundings and even on the darkest night will become visible to an infra-red sensor. As this device is completely passive the presence of the observer remains undetected. More serious is the fact that certain regions of the ship, notably the hull in the area of the machinery spaces and uptakes, are conspicuously warmer than the remainder and will tend to attract a heat-seeking anti-ship missile to one of the most vulnerable areas of the ship. Not only heat, but any type of energy radiation, such as injudicious use of radio, radar or active sonars, should be avoided. Silence remains golden.

Finally, a moving ship creates a three-dimensional pressure field in the water around her. On either beam it can cause interactive effects with nearby ships or banks and has resulted in some spectacular collisions over the years. Shallow water will cause a ship to 'squat', or trim by the stern. Simultaneously the water in the constricted space between ship and seabed is forced away, its increased velocity resulting in a pressure drop. This phenomenon can be made to flex a diaphragm to initiate the firing sequence of the most unsweepable of mines. It is not currently easy to simulate the pressure signature of a full-sized ship in order to detonate such mines harmlessly and the only safe course in waters thought to be contaminated is to reduce speed as far as possible.

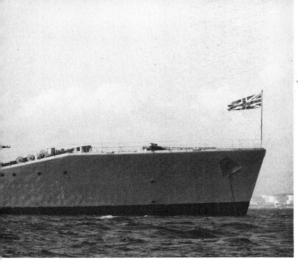

A warship's working environment is a compound of ocean and weather. Her purpose is to provide a reliable and steady weapons platform over a wide range of conditions and, beyond the seastate where she can still fight effectively, she still needs to survive. Good ship design practice cannot be safely subordinated to the demands of armament.

In a seaway, a ship moves in a complex manner, with up to six components. Three of these — pitch, roll and yaw — are rotations about the ship's three main axes; the other three — heave, surge and sway — are translations along the same axes. The degree of importance of any of these at any time depends on the characteristics of the ship, her course and speed, the sea conditions and even the wind. A quite violent tendency to movement can often be modified quite simply by an alteration of course or speed but sometimes it is more difficult. Extreme movement not only strains the ship and fatigues the crew but degrades the performance of the weapons systems requiring a stable reference plane.

Pitch causes large excursions and accelerations, greatest at the extremities of the ship and least at the pitch axis itself, somewhere abaft of amidships. Ideally, a flight pad and pitch-sensitive equipment should be sited in this neighbourhood. Pitch intensity is decided largely by the relationship between the length of the ship and the wavelength of a regular head sea; should they near-enough coincide and the ship's speed be critical, she can be 'tuned', getting into a synchronous pitch rhythm of exceptional severity, requiring remedial action. An undesirable feature of pitching is 'wetness' which is impossible to measure in absolute terms. At the low end of the scale, wetness takes the form of clouds of spray

Below left:
The ability of a submarine to remain concealed depends much upon how well she can use the non-uniform qualities of seawater and how well the AS ship is equipped to counter these effects. Much useful data on temperature, salinity and computed sound velocities is yielded by expandable bathythermographs and sound velocimetres. The spin-stabilised Sippican XBT shown, sinks rapidly, trailing a wire for the telemetering of data, a typical profile being also shown. *Sippican Ocean Systems Inc*

Below right:
Specified for the Canadian 'Halifax'-class frigates as well as Swedish ships, the Mk2 Bofors 57mm gun is housed in a new-style cupola which is profiled to give a low radar signature, vital primarily in defeating the active homer. With a rate of fire of 220 proximity-fused rounds/min and very low dispersion, the gun can tackle the missile itself. *AB Bofors*

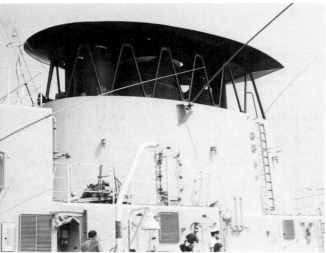

enveloping the forward end, rendering observation difficult and driving salt-laden moisture into every crevice. With increasingly severe pitching, solid water will also come aboard to the point where the ship 'takes it green' by responding too slowly to a head sea. Cracking and major structural damage may well result.

Deep inundation of bow shell plating causes external pressures which set it in. Usually it recovers on the upward movement, the process being graphically termed 'panting', but seams can be fatigued. Large movements forward also bring the forefoot, and sometimes a considerable length of bottom plating, clear of the water only to smash it down at the next plunge. Known as 'slamming' this process can permanently set-in the bottom and damage fixtures such as sonar domes. Heavy pitching will also bring the after end up, leaving the screws to race on a mixture of air and water.

Fine forward sections will encourage large amplitude of pitch but reduce deceleration rates. Increased freeboard will reduce wetness and this can sometimes be achieved simply by the addition of a forward bulwark, as in the American 'Knox' class frigates. A spray chine, even in the form of a simple metal strip, can be beneficial in throwing spray clear but a knuckle is more common in larger ships. This feature also allows a more pronounced flare without incurring excessive widths at upper deck level. Flare has the effect of rapidly increasing the water plane and therefore the buoyancy with submergence thus preventing the bows from burying themselves too deeply.

Where head seas cause one set of problems,

running 'down-hill' on a reciprocal course has hazards all of its own. Anyone who has helmed a dinghy in a blow will be familiar with the deceptive quietness of coming off the wind, the lightness in the tiller as a sea overtakes the boat, the resultant yaw and the automatic glance to the leach of the sail to see the first signs of lift prior to a gybe. In deep water, a well-ordered wave system can move at considerable velocity, dependent upon wavelength. For example, a sea of 150m (abour 500ft) peak to peak has wavefronts moving at about 30kt. Their normal height would be about 7.5m (about 25ft) but, if they were moving into shallower water, they would be getting progressively steeper until they would break. Breaking water is moving water and possesses considerable energy. A fast moving frigate of average length, about 122m, and running with the sea would slowly be overtaken by each wave in turn. She would be hazarded each time a breaking crest picked up the after end, for rudders and propellers lose effect in the moving water and the bows would be deeply immersed, acting as a brake. It is highly likely that the ship would be bodily rotated about the bows and laid broadside on to the sea, a situation of grave implication. The process, known as 'broaching', is signalled by yawing which becomes increasingly difficult to remedy and must be countered by a reduction in speed or a change in course. A smaller, high-powered vessel could probably even accelerate out of trouble.

Little has been achieved in the development of a method of reducing a ship's pitch in spite of continuing research. For an average-sized vessel, it is unlikely to exceed $\pm 7°$, though it may feel more, and it is possible only to stabilise those items of equipment that cannot tolerate pitch movement.

Roll, however, is a different matter. It can easily achieve an angle of five times that of pitch, once the sea is broad on the beam. An extremely stable ship responds rapidly to an imposed roll and will have a short, jerky period. A long, easy roll is unpleasant to a seaman for it demonstrates a small righting lever even though in some ships, such as aircraft carriers, side trawlers, RoRos, etc, it is an operational requirement. In these cases, the results of asymmetric flooding or the increase in topweight, for instance because of icing, must be taken into account during the design process.

Stabilisation against roll can be achieved by various means. Simplest, and very common, is the Bilge Keel, a metal strip projecting normally to the turn of the bilge on either side and running perhaps half a ship's length. Though quite effective, it adds to the wetted area and, therefore, the skin resistance of the ship. It may be replaced, or complemented by, one or more pairs of active fins which may, or may not, be retractable. Extending outward in the same plane as the bilge keel, they are of aerofoil section and may be rotated to provide lift. An inboard gyro unit senses

Below:
Possibly the current optimum gun calibre, considering range, rate of fire and hitting power is the 100mm. The Creusot-Loire mounting, seen here on the German-built Malaysian frigate *Lekir*, can select automatically from three types of ammunition and throw a 13.5kg projectile out to 17,500m. Elevation encompasses $-15°$ to $+80°$ and it will be noted how the gun's depression has demanded a reverse sheer right forward, resulting in wetness even in a moderate seastate. *Creusot-Loire Industrie*

the onset of a roll and turns the pair of fins to opposite angles, providing a powerful counter-couple.

It will be apparent that active fins need a flow over them to develop their lift force and will therefore become progressively less efficient with reduction in speed, having no effect when the ship is hove-to. Some ships, such as hydrographic survey vessels, need to spend considerable periods either stopped or moving slowly and tend therefore to be fitted with passive stabiliser tanks. In basic terms, these are a pair of deep tanks, sited amidships and with their bottoms connected athwartships by a duct. As the ship rolls water is transferred under gravity and its own momentum from one tank to the other. The duct forms a constriction which puts a phase delay in the process and, by careful calculation of the duct's cross-section, the movement can be made exactly anti-phase with the ship's natural roll, the kinetic energy of the moving water opposing that of the rolling ship. By added roll sensors and pumps, the system can be made active.

Yaw, mentioned above, is initiated through wind and sea being from a broad angle on the bow or

Above:
As extra hazard for today's thin-skinned ships is surface ice. Here the Canadian replenishment ship HMCS *Protecteur* is seen in broken pack ice. Even the thickness of these small floes would menace a frigate's hull, endanger her propellers and sonar dome, and effectively prevent the streaming of any other sensors. *Canadian Armed Forces*

Right:
Associated with the SQS 505 VDS, is a towed body over 5m in length. Seen here on a Canadian DDH, the body is deployed over a gantry in the stern well and extreme care is necessary when handling it in poor conditions. Note how the cable, paid-out separately over the sheave, is fitted with anti-strum fairing to reduce self-noise. *Canadian Armed Forces*

quarter. Wave profiles along either side of the ship will be different but varying regularly at a rate which is a function of ship and wave velocity. The upshot is that the centres of pressure on either side move in a rhythmic relationship that produces a significant rotational effect above the ship's vertical axis, pushing her alternately one side, then the other, of her set course. An autopilot will correct for these movements but, as they need to be initiated before a corrective rudder angle can be applied, the latter may need to be quite large, absorbing much power and wearing the steering gear. Predictive autopilots are being developed to improve response.

Heave is the vertical translation of the ship, a bodily movement analogous to the bobbing of a cork and, theoretically at least, possible without either roll or pitch. Though it poses one more input for a firing solution, it is very difficult to quantify except as a

derivative of vertical acceleration. Momentarily, when the ship has been lifted dynamically and is on the crest of a sea, she will experience a decrease in stability.

Surge is the forward augmentation in speed caused by an overtaking sea. Sway is the sideways equivalent. Neither is of much consequence.

All these natural forces, to say nothing of the effects of windage on superstructure, work continuously on a ship and 'seakindliness' is the ability to function efficiently and comfortably in spite of them. To predict how a proposed hull will react to its

environment, a naval architect has a powerful tool in model testing in a specialist ship tank facility. Experiments combine the predictive — which influence the final design — and the retrospective, where full-scale trials are carried out in the resultant ship to check the correctness of the earlier model tests. The process is thus one of continuous refinement.

A basic requirement is to determine the resistance of a full to being driven through the water. An accurate model, of wax or GRP and about 5m in length is therefore towed beneath a carriage running the length of a specialist tank. By connecting the model through a dynamometer the resistance of the bare hull is determined. For a surface ship this is composed primarily of skin friction and wave-making resistance. As the former element can be calculated separately and fairly accurately, the latter can also be derived and scaled up for a figure for the full-sized hull.

A similar model is run with a speed-controlled motor, shafts, propellers and other appendages added. Thrust and torque are monitored over a series of runs, the propellers then being tested in open water to obtain characteristics unmodified by model flow. A larger model of the propeller is meanwhile being exhaustively checked in a cavitation tunnel where its design can be refined to minimise cavitation or confine its onset to points outside critical speed bands. Flow over the hull can also be observed in a circulating water channel (the marine equivalent of a wind tunnel) where lines and appendages can be optimised to minimum turbulence. These experiments may produce a clean and easily-driven hull but will not prove its manoeuvrability or behaviour in a seaway.

A self-contained and highly-instrumented model is therefore run in a manoeuvring tank. Battery-powered and radio controlled, this model is correctly trimmed and ballasted. It is put through a comprehensive series of checks including straight runs, circles at various rudder angles, spirals and zig-zags to thoroughly check the response of the model over its whole speed range. 'Pull-out' manoeuvres will define its directional stability. Shortcomings in these experiments will result in modifications to rudder shape, size or position and, possibly, to the underwater body itself. The manoeuvring tank is deep enough to allow submerged submarine models to be run in addition to surface ships.

The final refinement of the tank is a bank of wave-makers which, with variation of the period and amplitude of strokes, can create a desired sea of the correct scale. As many manoeuvres as are deemed necessary can be repeated in various patterns of sea to establish the seakindliness of a design before the expensive stage of cutting metal begins.

Below:
With their very fine forward sections and large bow sonar bulb, the American 'Knox' class frigates were widely criticised for their wetness forward. At the cost of inhibiting the gun in depression the freeboard has been raised with a bulwark right forward, as here in the *Moinester*. Note also the spray rail. *Mike Lennon*

CHAPTER 9

The Future

What then of the future in warship development? As ever, lobbies abound. Some advocate an all-submarine fleet, others a 'high-tech' navy with exotic hull forms and advanced engineering. Some stress airpower, others the various forms of force projection. All will advance good reasons for their conviction, but all too often examination of these and their relation to the broader canvas of maritime warfare will reveal either vested interest or blinkered outlook. Most, if not all, have a place in any fleet worthy of the name but each must be complemented by the others, the whole balanced to meet its flag's commitments into a realistic future.

A fleet is analogous to the full orchestra. Neglect the brass and Berlioz will be beyond it, sloppy strings will reduce the technical excellence of a Mendelssohn to nought. Small-scale sinofonietta and chamber works require the formation and training of elite groups, while top quality specialists must be made available for concerto performances. Certain instrumentalists must be able to tackle alternative roles for less conventional pieces. Beyond the actual performance, the corporate whole needs sound organisation and management together with a conductor who can bully or cajole but, above all, lead while understanding the strengths and limitations of his players in relation to the work in hand.

So with a fleet. A C-in-C needs to know that he has the commited backing of the political and organisational establishments. He may exercise in trade protection or surface action, in survival against submarine or aircraft, yet still find himself wanting in the teeth of a minelaying campaign. As the orchestra must rehearse exhaustively if it would seek perfection, so must the fleet admiral exercise endlessly to weld his force into a coherent fighting weapon. Constant exercise is expensive however, not least in wear and tear on the ships themselves, and is therefore unpopular with parsimonious treasuries. With ever-tighter budgets and constantly-changing threats there has to be flexibility in thought, a feeling for the making of economies without an attendant reduction in standards and an ability to make change without doing so for its own sake.

Defence costs in the face of a common threat from a superpower can be spread by the formation of international alliances, such as NATO, SEATO or the Warsaw Pact. Unfortunately, where it can be argued fairly convincingly that such alliances reduce the likelihood of war, there is little hard evidence on how well they function once conflict is actually entered into. In 1940, for instance, Great Britain had powerful maritime friends, but had she modelled and limited her own fleet on the assumption that their ships would have been available in war, she would have lost the war at sea and as a consequence the war itself. For when it mattered these fleets were not available — not because they had been destroyed but because in some cases the states to which they belonged were neutral or had been defeated militarily and in others the fleets were simply needed elsewhere. History demonstrates how national interests tend to emerge from within international taskings or how the latter fail through lack of mutual comprehension. ABDA failed against the Japanese in 1942 mainly through lack of common precedures — these led to reverses that sapped morale to the extent that the force lacked success even when it could muster local superiority. The much vaunted triumph of international co-operation in the Medterranean landings of World War 2 was largely politically cosmetic. Even Korea is not a reliable yardstick, being essentially a war fought by maritime powers, uncontested at sea, against a land power. Though NATO has doubtless improved things considerably there is still plenty of evidence of national interest and lack of urgency in standardisation, even when obviously in the organisation's interests. To have any real chance of surviving a sustained non-nuclear war, Great Britain should not only remain committed to NATO but also to the sea, retaining a fully autonomous and capable navy and mercantile marine. Locked to, and dependent upon, a militarily-minded Europe — however advantageous the arrangements in peace — she may ultimately sink with it. Great Britain is as much an island as she ever was, still far from self-sufficiency. Reliable sources and a strong independent fleet to guarantee their delivery are still vital, for when the heat really comes on the bonds of alliances tend to weaken and melt. Governments ignore these basic facts for short term political gain; to reabsorb them all too often involves hostilities.

If alliances there have to be, the financial strictures

that justify their existence shoud justify also a high degree of standardisation. Two basic types of frigate would suit the needs of all NATO navies, yet most design and build their own. Likewise two types of conventional submarine and possibly three of mine warfare ships would suffice, yet again there is a plethora of designs. Each country, though wedded to an alliance, strongly desires to retain an independent capability across the board; if these national interests are so evident in peace, they can only be accentuated in war.

Assuming then that a fleet insists on funding its own expensively exclusive designs, it surely makes sense to adopt a more committed approach to develop those whose weapon and sensor fits can be changed with minimum upheaval to suit a variety of missions. Both the USA and Britain have toyed for years with the idea of interchangeability but have always stressed the penalties rather than the potential gains. Not surprisingly, years of such negative thought have produced nothing but paper while it has been left to German private enterprise to demonstate that the MEKO is not only possible but very exportable. As discussed in Chapter 8, it could spread and ease procurement costs, and guarantee that ships geared predominantly to, say, ASW never again need to be sunk by low-level bombing because their weapon fits were unsuitable for the occasion. Repair by replacement should mean substantially lower proportions of a warship's life being spent under refit; utilisation factors should improve and result in an effectively larger fleet. If so high a level of use

demands relief crews (as in SSBNs) this should promote few difficulties with a government keen to get an ever higher proportion of an ever dwindling total of uniformed men to sea.

Does a warship need to *look* like a warship? As we have seen, volume is at a premium, high speed is no longer so vital and costs are of disproportionately high importance. In recent years mercantile hulls have become infinitely more efficient, mainly due to the stimulus of rocketing bunker prices. A current 110m open-hulled container ship would, for instance, be powered and designed for a service speed of little over 20kts; why not a government-funded alternative with lines refined for, say, 24kts? Some loss of cubic capacity would result and further space would need to

be devoted to the extra 80% or so power that would be required, but such ships could be bareboat-chartered in peacetime to commercial operators as long as both parties had agreed on design parameters that suited their joint objectives. In times of heightened tension, and periodically for training of reserve manpower, they could be withdrawn from service and their container cells utilised for modular weapon systems. For instance a semi-width hatch may well be three ISO containers wide and two long, with an underdeck capacity four containers deep. This represents a carefully engineered and rigid space some 80ft (24.37m) long, 24ft (7.31m) wide and 32ft (9.75m) deep, one of six such on board. Vertical-launch missile systems lend themselves very well to being engineered into a single-piece module which, pre-tested and fresh from store could be slotted into place in minutes by any modern shipyard with a 500-tonne crane.

The *Arapaho* project has demonstrated how such ships can also act as helicopter or V/STOL carriers. Again, a medium-sized container ship has been used, her large pontoon hatch covers overlaid by light-weight deck segments for the flight operations of six Sea Kings, whose garaging, maintenance, generating, stores and even crew accommodation have been built

into ISO-dimensioned containers, grouped as required.

It is essential that this experiment is a success, not only to prove the feasibility of producing a viable auxiliary warship but also to demonstrate that such a ship has a capacity for self-defence. The size and speed of very large container ships enable them to outstrip any but the best surface escorts in a seaway, while they are not suitable candidates for convoy. At the same time, their value and scarcity would make each loss a disaster. A helicopter flight topsides would not detract from underdeck cargo capacity, yet would provide defence against a marauding high-speed submarine with anti-ship missiles. Containerised lightweight point-defence SAM systems, such as the proven and available Sea Wolf, together with CIWS rapid fire guns and both aerial and towed decoys should also be available together with specialist crews. If necessary, the whole outfit can be transferred from a ship leaving a high-risk zone to another ship about to enter it.

Should a force of auxiliary warships and hybrid merchantmen be properly funded and organised in peacetime, much work could be undertaken by civil shipyards in place of royal dockyards debilitated and abandoned by government defence plans. British Aerospace have produced a whole family of systems to achieve this end. Known as SCADS (Shipborne Containerised Air Defence Systems) they should be acquired and thoroughly evaluated in peace, for there will be little enough time in war.

Superfluous tankers or bulk carriers (currently available at prices little better than their scrap value) could be acquired to serve as 'Aunt Sallies'. The Gulf

Above:
Return of the 'Great White Whale'. For the Falklands War in 1982, *Canberra* was one of just a handful of liners left to Great Britain as troop transports. The superb co-operation between the Red and White ensigns has been poorly rewarded by a Government apparently ignorant of the significance of seapower. *Mike Lennon*

Right:
Future victors at sea will likely be those that have best invested in technology. The Soviet Union has a large auxiliary fleet of ocean research ships and range trackers such as the *Kosmonaut Victor Patsayev*, built on a very German hull and seen here in the Scheldt. *L & L van Ginderen*

Below right:
Technology with a difference in the British seabed operations vessel (SOV) *Challenger*. With saturation diving, moonpool and diving bell, manned submersibles and dynamic positioning the ship can undertake a wide variety of missions in the deep oceans. *L & L van Ginderen*

War has demonstrated repeatedly the powers of survival of loaded or inerted VLCCs against strikes from large air-launched missiles. Though rather slow, such a ship, with all tanks secured and equipped with a variety of suitable lures, could accompany a task group. Any unexpected incoming anti-ship missiles would be provied with a target hard to resist, leaving high-value ships to deal only with 'strays'. Though the idea may sound suicidal, a precedent exists in the German 'Sperrbrecher' of World War 2, used to blast a path through a minefield.

It is not argued that a whole new fleet could be conjured from nowhere overnight, that it would cost peanuts or that an auxiliary can be anywhere near as useful as a regular warship. But such a force could be used in lower-risk areas, freeing frontline warships for higher-grade duties. There are centuries of tradition behind merchantmen at war; they have provided many a stopgap solution and could do so again if Britain's maritime policy were to value the fleet rather than to run it down or drive it under flags of convenience.

Could a few 'high-tech' ships replace greater numbers of conventional warships? Though at the time of writing this looks doubtful, several types of 'exotic' would seem to have their own roles.

As discussed earlier, speed is still a valid requirement in small, agile craft, the SSM-armed FAC being the modern equivalent of the 'torpedo boat' that appeared such a threat at the turn of the century. Similarities include relative cheapness, a potentially giant-killing armament and ready deployment by the aspiring navy with few basic skills. A further parallel, however, could lie in the ability of those threatened to produce an antidote. Speed is the small warship's defence and can be improved considerably by lifting the hull partially, or completely, clear of the water. The classic method is by configuring the underside of the hull in flat 'V' sections which, with a suitably-located centre of gravity, will impart lift with forward motion, causing the hull to rise in the water and lose much of its skin and wavemaking resistance. Though still valid, this

Out of her element, PHM 4 *Aquila* looks cumbersome with her bow and stern foils in the retracted position. She can proceed at 11kts in this 'boating' mode, powered by two low-powered, diesel-driven waterjets. The foils are obviously vulnerable to damage in this state and manoeuvrability has therefore been enhanced by a side-thruster, whose aperture is visible below the forward draught marks.
Boeing Marine Systems

Above right:
***Aries* at speed with foils lowered.** *Boeing Marine Systems*

type of hull-form rapidly loses performance with deteriorating conditions and has lost popularity in favour of round-bilged hulls, which are slower but more seakindly. Even so, the fast 'mosquito' craft is still useful in the disputing of narrow-seas choke-points and the drawbacks of the hard-chine, high-speed hull can be mitigated by the use of hydrofoils, either in an auxiliary capacity or as fully-fledged appendages.

Hydrofoils usually have a 'V'-form hull, equipped fore and aft with struts that support the foils, which may be surface-piercing or fully submerged. The former offer continuity of support and an effective area dependent upon craft speed but project vulnerably and permanently. The latter can be attached to struts that can be elevated from the water when required. Proceeding at low speeds the hydrofoil is hullborne, (the 'boating' mode), driven usually by a conventional marine propeller. She needs to be able to achieve sufficient forward velocity to create the foil-lift necessary to raise the hull clear of the water whereupon propulsive power is developed usually by waterjet units, which obviate the need for noisy and complex drive shafts. Some Chinese craft have foils only as aids, lifting the hull in the water but not out of it.

Once foilborne, the craft can enjoy a smooth 'ride' even in quite severe sea states. Sophisticated sensor systems in the foils detect their instantaneous submergence and operate servo-controlled flaps at angles and rates that take account of the dynamic characteristics of the craft.

For the Italian navy the hydrofoil is not only useful for the control of the central Mediterranean narrows but also does not suffer from its major drawback, its poor endurance, because of the short distances involved. The British, on the other hand, saw its possibilities in fast-response policing of the offshore EEZ: for this, they purchased and evaluated a Jetfoil but, though successful, the trials showed that the large degree of necessary support was justified only if a fleet of such craft were to be employed.

Though it is technically feasible to construct a frigate-sized hydrofoil craft, it would seem at present to offer little advantage over a conventional ship while being considerably more expensive. Currently,

the full benefits of the hydrofoil princpile can be realised only on a small scale. The hovercraft, or Surface Effect Ship (SES), may work out more cheaply but her mandatory light alloy hull is more subject to severe shock from high speed wave contact and structural damage is more common. Riding on an airbubble contained within its flexible skirt or rigid sidewall, it is an efficient user of energy and is able to hover at zero speed. With flexible skirts it is a true amphibian, capable of working over any reasonably regular flat surface, be it water, marsh or land. Deteriorating sea conditions find its performance rapidly degraded but it has the great advantage of low water-transmitted signatures. Not surprisingly, therefore, the hovercraft currently looks most promising in the roles of fast assault and mine counter-measures. Each requires a short, wide plan which, though weather vulnerable, is best at high speeds. To develop the SES concept further, to give it a deep-sea role, requires a project as bold as the US Navy's recent 2,000-ton proposal which unfortunately fell victim to the axe of economy. This frigate-sized craft would have been longer and narrower, accepting the lower probable 50kt maximum speed as a reasonable trade-off against much improved seakeeping. Though, like hydrofoils, flexibly-skirted hovercraft are elevated above the water surface, they are usually propelled by airscrews which even when ducted make them extremely noisy but enable them to manoeuvre ashore where waterjets obviously cannot be used.

Pre-revolutionary Iran purchased BH7 hovercraft for use in the fast attack role although compared with the conventional FAC they were more expensive, noisier, required more maintenance, carried less armament, had inferior endurance and presented a large radar profile with hotspots. Their advantages were a 65kt speed (compared with the average FAC's 38kts), an ability to disregard shallows when planning an attack and the possibilities of setting-up an advanced base on any convenient beach.

As MCMVs hovercraft have shown a high immunity to both detection and explosion though, like hydrofoils, they require comprehensive support facilities. At the time of writing, it looks as though the Americans will be the first to exploit the hovercraft's potential against mines.

A further advantage of the short SES is its deck area which is large in relation to its length and valuable to a ship dedicated to helicopter operations. The latter would benefit from range rather than outright speed, so a multi-hull ship could be adopted to achieve the same ends, probably in the form of a catamaran (ie with two parallel hulls bridged by a flat deck). While the wetted area must increase, the hulls can be made much finer; the net result is that the additional skin resistance is offset by reduced wave-making resistance and only little more installed power is required. Undamaged, the catamaran form is immensely stable and is not prone to rolling at low speeds, when active stabilisation is none too effective.

Assymetric flooding would, however, require prompt and carefully-considered counter-flooding. The layout lends itself to specialist heavy lifters or research ships such as the US Navy's *Hayes* (T-AGOR-16) and the Australian's new 'Bay' class MCMVs, GRP catamarans whose deck area is exploited for sweep and hunting gear.

Convincing cases have been made for frigate-sized escorts dedicated to carrying and operating six LAMPS-type helicopters. A multi-hull would here be essential but for ocean use could well be improved by adopting the SWATH principle. This, the Small Waterplane Area Twin-Hulled ship, in place of two more or less conventional hulls, has its deck platform supported on pylons, or two very narrow structures sited atop two fully-submerged submarine-like bodies that provide the greater part of the buoyancy and house the propulsion systems. While sharing the advantages of the catarmaran, the SWATH promises improved seakeeping as the main buoyant elements are submerged well below the effects of surface conditions which, in turn, have little effect on the

pylons which possess little inherent buoyancy. With its large wetted areas, the SWATH will be propulsivley less efficient than a conventional craft at low speeds but at high speeds, where wave-making resistance is of greater significance, her overall efficiency improves. For the benefits of a half hectare of deck space the penalty of some extra installed power may well prove a good investment.

A potentially interesting area for investigation is the Wing-in-Ground (WIG) vehicle. This occupies the middle ground between air and marine craft, being neither the one nor the other. Early prototypes have looked rather like large, stubby-proportioned aircraft with wings and vectored-thrust power units. Suitably configured it can use either land or water for take-off and landing, gaining height at low speeds by the use of downthrust. Forward motion imparts lift and the engines are gradually revectored for forward thrust. Unlike an aircraft, it does not continue to climb but flies low to retain what may be viewed as a rolling bubble of air between the earth's surface and its underside. This 'bubble' supplies much of the WIG's lift so that its own surfaces can be relatively small in area and thus in drag. Suitably developed, the principle may be the means of propelling quite large vehicles or payloads. Like the hovercraft they could be fully amphibious and, while they would lack the ability to hover, they would 'fly' at heights suitable for the negotiation of seas or obstacles beyond the capabilities of the hovercraft. Soviet interest in what they have termed the 'Ekranoplan' seems centred on its use in the assault mode but, suitably armed, it would appear to have a future in surface ship attack roles.

Moving even further toward the true aircraft is the airship. A new generation is at last evolving, free of the stigmas cast by early craft with their hydrogen gas, heavy framing and poor engines. Capable of carrying significant payloads with long endurance, it could have roles in reconnaissance, ASW and early warning. For AS work it could hover almost indefinitely and have smaller signatures than a helicopter. Though airships were used in both wars their contributions were not large. Current experiments may reveal its true role at sea.

The displacement ship will always have the advantage when it comes to endurance and capacity, and is unlikely to be superseded in the foreseeable future. However, despite all the technological advances, it still consists basically of a hull propelled by long shafts that drive marine propellers. Though obviously considerably improved, these remain the components of the warship of a century ago. It is tempting to see the propulsion system replaced universally by, say, water jets or vectored-thrust units, as discussed in Chapter 3, but these still offer no real advantages except in particular cases.

Nevertheless, fish are not propelled by any such devices and, while the forward thrust imparted by the sculling action of the tail is unlikely to be capable of imitation in any man-made craft, it is not beyond possibility that outer skins could be made flexible and energised over a large area to parallel the fish's muscular thrust. Such an arrangement would also offer the chance to exist in harmony with the waterflow rather than eternally battling against it.

What seems certain is that the warship tends to evolve slowly in peacetime and only the war that she was built to deter provides the economic justification for radical leaps forward.

7/05^{12}

8/94^8 1/98$"$